CLOUD COMPUTING 2023

The Fourteenth International Conference on Cloud Computing, GRIDs, and Virtualization

June 26 - 30, 2023

Nice, France

CLOUD COMPUTING 2023 Editors

Andreas Aßmuth, Ostbayerische Technische Hochschule Amberg-Weiden, Germany

Printed from e-media with permission by:

Curran Associates, Inc.
57 Morehouse Lane
Red Hook, NY 12571

Some format issues inherent in the e-media version may also appear in this print version.

Printed with permission by Curran Associates, Inc. (2024)

International Academy, Research, and Industry Association (IARIA)
412 Derby Way
Wilmington, DE 19810

Phone: (408) 893-6407
Fax: (408) 527-6351

petre@iaria.org

Additional copies of this publication are available from:

Curran Associates, Inc.
57 Morehouse Lane
Red Hook, NY 12571 USA
Phone: 845-758-0400
Fax: 845-758-2633
Email: curran@proceedings.com
Web: www.proceedings.com

Table of Contents

CLOUD COMPUTING 2023

Forward

The Fourteenth International Conference on Cloud Computing, GRIDs, and Virtualization (CLOUD COMPUTING 2023), held on June 26 - 30, 2023, continued a series of events targeted to prospect the applications supported by the new paradigm and validate the techniques and the mechanisms. A complementary target was to identify the open issues and the challenges to fix them, especially on security, privacy, and inter- and intra-clouds protocols.

Cloud computing is a normal evolution of distributed computing combined with Service-oriented architecture, leveraging most of the GRID features and Virtualization merits. The technology foundations for cloud computing led to a new approach of reusing what was achieved in GRID computing with support from virtualization.

The conference had the following tracks:

- Cloud computing
- Computing in virtualization-based environments
- Platforms, infrastructures and applications
- Challenging features
- New Trends
- Grid networks, services and applications

Similar to the previous edition, this event attracted excellent contributions and active participation from all over the world. We were very pleased to receive top quality contributions.

We take here the opportunity to warmly thank all the members of the CLOUD COMPUTING 2023 technical program committee, as well as the numerous reviewers. The creation of such a high quality conference program would not have been possible without their involvement. We also kindly thank all the authors that dedicated much of their time and effort to contribute to CLOUD COMPUTING 2023. We truly believe that, thanks to all these efforts, the final conference program consisted of top quality contributions.

Also, this event could not have been a reality without the support of many individuals, organizations and sponsors. We also gratefully thank the members of the CLOUD COMPUTING 2023 organizing committee for their help in handling the logistics and for their work that made this professional meeting a success.

We hope that CLOUD COMPUTING 2023 was a successful international forum for the exchange of ideas and results between academia and industry and to promote further progress in the area of cloud computing, GRIDs and virtualization. We also hope that Nce provided a pleasant environment during the conference and everyone saved some time to enjoy this beautiful city.

CLOUD COMPUTING 2023 Steering Committee

CLOUD COMPUTING 2023 Publicity Chair

CLOUD COMPUTING 2023

Committee

CLOUD COMPUTING 2023 Steering Committee

Carlos Becker Westphall, Federal University of Santa Catarina, Brazil
Yong Woo Lee, University of Seoul, Korea
Bob Duncan, University of Aberdeen, UK
Alex Sim, Lawrence Berkeley National Laboratory, USA
Sören Frey, Daimler TSS GmbH, Germany
Andreas Aßmuth, Ostbayerische Technische Hochschule (OTH) Amberg-Weiden, Germany
Uwe Hohenstein, Siemens AG, Germany
Magnus Westerlund, Arcada, Finland
Aspen Olmsted, College of Charleston, USA

CLOUD COMPUTING 2023 Publicity Chair

José Miguel Jiménez, Universitat Politecnica de Valencia, Spain
Sandra Viciano Tudela, Universitat Politecnica de Valencia, Spain

CLOUD COMPUTING 2023 Technical Program Committee

Omar Aaziz, Sandia National Laboratories, USA
Sherif Abdelwahed, Virginia Commonwealth University, USA
Vibhatha Abeykoon, Voltron Data Inc., USA
Maruf Ahmed, The University of Technology, Sydney, Australia
Mubashwir Alam, Marquette University, USA
Abdulelah Alwabel, Prince Sattam Bin Abdulaziz University, Kingdom of Saudi Arabia
Mário Antunes, Polytechnic of Leiria, Portugal
Filipe Araujo, University of Coimbra, Portugal
Andreas Aßmut, Ostbayerische Technische Hochschule (OTH) Amberg-Weiden, Germany
Odiljon Atabaev, Andijan Machine-Building Institute, Uzbekistan
Babak Badnava, University of Kansas, USA
Luis-Eduardo Bautista-Villalpando, Autonomous University of Aguascalientes, Mexico
Carlos Becker Westphall, Federal University of Santa Catarina, Brazil
Mehdi Belkhiria, University of Rennes 1 | IRISA | Inria, France
Leila Ben Ayed, National School of Computer Science | University of Manouba, Tunisia
Nicola Bena, Università degli Studi di Milano, Italy
Salima Benbernou, Universite Paris Cite, France
Andreas Berl, Technische Hochschule Deggendorf, Germany
Simona Bernardi, University of Zaragoza, Spain
Dixit Bhatta, University of Delaware, USA
Constantinos Bitsakos, National Technical University of Athens, Greece

Peter Bloodsworth, University of Oxford, UK
Jalil Boukhobza, University of Western Brittany, France
Marco Brocanelli, Wayne State University, USA
Antonio Brogi, University of Pisa, Italy
Roberta Calegari, Alma Mater Studiorum-Università di Bologna,Italy
Paolo Campegiani, Bit4id, Italy
Juan Vicente Capella Hernández, Universitat Politècnica de València, Spain
Roberto Casadei, Alma Mater Studiorum - Università di Bologna, Italy
Víctor Casamayor, TU Vienna, Austria
Adithya Rajesh Chandrassery, National Institute of Technology Karnataka, Surathkal, India
Ruay-Shiung Chang, National Taipei University of Business, Taipei, Taiwan
Ryan Chard, Argonne National Laboratory, USA
Batyr Charyyev, Stevens Institute of Technology, USA
Hao Che, University of Texas at Arlington, USA
Yitao Chen, Arizona State University, USA
Yue Cheng, George Mason University, USA
Claudio Cicconetti, National Research Council, Italy
Daniel Corujo, Universidade de Aveiro | Instituto de Telecomunicações, Portugal
Patrizio Dazzi, University of Pisa, Italy
Noel De Palma, University Grenoble Alpes, France
Mª del Carmen Carrión Espinosa, University of Castilla-La Mancha, Spain
Chen Ding, Ryerson University, Canada
Karim Djemame, University of Leeds, UK
Ramon dos Reis Fontes, Federal University of Rio Grande do Norte, Natal, Brazil
Bob Duncan, University of Aberdeen, UK
Steve Eager, University West of Scotland, UK
Nabil El Ioini, Free University of Bolzano, Italy
Rania Fahim El-Gazzar, Universty of South-Eastern Norway, Norway
Ibrahim El-Shekeil, Metropolitan State University, USA
Levent Ertaul, California State University, East Bay, USA
Javier Fabra, Universidad de Zaragoza, Spain
Fairouz Fakhfakh, University of Sfax, Tunisia
Hamid M. Fard, Technical University of Darmstadt, Germany
Umar Farooq, University of California, Riverside, USA
Tadeu Ferreira Oliveira, Federal Institute of Science Education and Technology of Rio Grande do Norte, Brazil
Jan Fesl, Institute of Applied Informatics - University of South Bohemia, Czech Republic
Sebastian Fischer, University of Applied Sciences OTH Regensburg, Germany
Kaneez Fizza, Swinburne University of Technology, Australia
Stefano Forti, University of Pisa, Italy
Sören Frey, Daimler TSS GmbH, Germany
Somchart Fugkeaw, Sirindhorn International Institute of Technology | Thammasat University, Thailand
Katja Gilly, Miguel Hernandez University, Spain
Jing Gong, KTH, Sweden
Poonam Goyal, Birla Institute of Technology & Science, Pilani, India
Nils Gruschka, University of Oslo, Norway
Jordi Guitart, Universitat Politècnica de Catalunya - Barcelona Supercomputing Center, Spain
Saurabh Gupta, Graphic Era Deemed to be University, Dehradun, India

Seif Haridi, KTH/SICS, Sweden
Herodotos Herodotou, Cyprus University of Technology, Cyprus
Uwe Hohenstein, Siemens AG Munich, Germany
Soamar Homsi, Air Force Research Laboratory (AFRL), USA
Md Rajib Hossen, The University of Texas at Arlington, USA
Anca Daniela Ionita, University Politehnica of Bucharest, Romania
Mohammad Atiqul Islam, The University of Texas at Arlington, USA
Saba Jamalian, Roosevelt University / Braze, USA
Fuad Jamour, University of California, Riverside, USA
Weiwei Jia, New Jersey Institute of Technology, USA
Carlos Juiz, University of the Balearic Islands, Spain
Sokratis Katsikas, Norwegian University of Science and Technology, Norway
Attila Kertesz, University of Szeged, Hungary
Zaheer Khan, University of the West of England, Bristol, UK
Ioannis Konstantinou, CSLAB - NTUA, Greece
Sonal Kumari, Samsung R&D Institute, India
Van Thanh Le, Free University of Bozen-Bolzano, Italy
Yong Woo Lee, University of Seoul, Korea
Sarah Lehman, Temple University, USA
Kunal Lillaney, Amazon Web Services, USA
Enjie Liu, University of Bedfordshire, UK
Pinglan Liu, Iowa State University, USA
Xiaodong Liu, Edinburgh Napier University, UK
Jay Lofstead, Sandia National Laboratories, USA
Hui Lu, Binghamton University (State University of New York), USA
Weibin Ma, University of Delaware, USA
Hosein Mohammadi Makrani, University of California, Davis, USA
Shaghayegh Mardani, University of California Los Angeles (UCLA), USA
Stefano Mariani, University of Modena and Reggio Emilia, Italy
Attila Csaba Marosi, Institute for Computer Science and Control - Hungarian Academy of Sciences, Hungary
Romolo Marotta, University of l'Aquila (UNIVAQ), Italy
Antonio Matencio Escolar, University West of Scotland, UK
Jean-Marc Menaud, IMT Atlantique, France
Philippe Merle, Inria, France
Nasro Min-Allah, Imam Abdulrahman Bin Faisal University (IAU), KSA
Preeti Mishra, Graphic Era Deemed to be University, Dehradun, India
Takashi Miyamura, NTT Network Service Systems Labs, Japan
Francesc D. Muñoz-Escoí, Universitat Politècnica de València, Spain
Ioannis Mytilinis, National Technical University of Athens, Greece
Tamer Nadeem, Virginia Commonwealth University, USA
Hidemoto Nakada, National Institute of Advanced Industrial Science and Technology (AIST), Japan
Akash Nayak, IBM Research, India
Antonio Nehme, Birmingham City University, UK
Richard Neill, RN Technologies LLC, USA
Jens Nicolay, Vrije Universiteit Brussel, Belgium
Ridwan Rashid Noel, Texas Lutheran University, USA
Alexander Norta, Tallinn Technology University, Estonia

Aspen Olmsted, Simmons University, USA
Matthias Olzmann, noventum consulting GmbH - Münster, Germany
Brajendra Panda, University of Arkansas, USA
Lorena Parra, Universitat Politècnica de València, Spain
Arnab K. Paul, BITS Pilani, India
Alessandro Pellegrini, National Research Council (CNR), Italy
Sathya Peri, Indian Institute of Technology Hyderabad, India
Nancy Perrot, Orange Innovation, France
Tamas Pflanzner, University of Szeged, Hungary
Paulo Pires, Fluminense Federal University (UFF), Brazil
Agostino Poggi, Università degli Studi di Parma, Italy
Saul E. Pomares Hernandez, Instituto Nacional de Astrofísica, Óptica y Electrónica Tonantzintla, Puebla, Mexico / SARA Group, LAAS-CNRS, Toulouse, France
Pavana Prakash, University of Houston, USA
Walter Priesnitz Filho, Federal University of Santa Maria, Rio Grande do Sul, Brazil
Abena Primo, Huston-Tillotson University, USA
Mohammed A Qadeer, Aligarh Muslim University, India
George Qiao, KLA, USA
Zhihao Qu, Hohai University, China
Francesco Quaglia, University of Rome Tor Vergata, Italy
M. Mustafa Rafique, Rochester Institute of Technology, USA
Danda B. Rawat, Howard University, USA
Daniel A. Reed, University of Utah, USA
Christoph Reich, Hochschule Furtwangen University, Germany
Eduard Gibert Renart, Rutgers Unversity, USA
Sashko Ristov, University of Innsbruck, Austria
Javier Rocher Morant, Universitat Politecnica de Valencia, Spain
Ivan Rodero, Rutgers University, USA
Takfarinas Saber, University College Dublin, Ireland
Mohamed Aymen Saied, Laval University, Canada
Rabia Saleem, University of Derby, UK
Hemanta Sapkota, University of Nevada - Reno, USA
Benjamin Schwaller, Sandia National Laboratories, USA
Savio Sciancalepore, TU Eindhoven, Netherlands
Wael Sellami, Higher Institute of Computer Sciences of Mahdia - ReDCAD laboratory, Tunisia
Jianchen Shan, Hofstra University, USA
Larisa Shwartz, T.J. Watson Research Center IBM, USA
Muhammad Abu Bakar Siddique, University of California, Riverside, USA
Altino Manuel Silva Sampaio, Escola Superior de Tecnologia e Gestão | Instituto Politécnico do Porto, Portugal
Alex Sim, Lawrence Berkeley National Laboratory, USA
Bowen Song, University of Southern California, USA
Hui Song, SINTEF, Norway
Vasily Tarasov, IBM Research, USA
Zahir Tari, School of Computing Technologies | RMIT University, Australia
Bedir Tekinerdogan, Wageningen University, The Netherlands
Parimala Thulasiraman, University of Manitoba, Canada
Orazio Tomarchio, University of Catania, Italy

Copyright Information

Encrypted Container File: Design and Implementation of a Hybrid-Encrypted Multi-Recipient File Structure

Tobias J. Bauer and Andreas Aßmuth
Ostbayerische Technische Hochschule Amberg-Weiden
Faculty of Electrical Engineering, Media and Computer Science
Kaiser-Wilhelm-Ring 23, 92224 Amberg, Germany
Email: {t.bauer|a.assmuth}@oth-aw.de

***Abstract*—Modern software engineering trends towards Cloud-native software development by international teams of developers. Cloud-based version management services, such as GitHub, are used for the source code and other artifacts created during the development process. However, using such a service usually means that every developer has access to all data stored on the platform. Particularly, if the developers belong to different companies or organizations, it would be desirable for sensitive files to be encrypted in such a way that these can only be decrypted again by a group of previously defined people. In this paper, we examine currently available tools that address this problem, but which have certain shortcomings. We then present our own solution, Encrypted Container Files (ECF), for this problem, eliminating the deficiencies found in the other tools.**

***Keywords*—Cloud-based software development; hybrid encryption; agile software engineering.**

I. Introduction

Software development undergoes a permanent change and, occasionally, long-lasting trends emerge, which influence the choices made in terms of software architectures, technologies, programming languages and frameworks used. Current trends involve the development of Cloud-native distributed software components which are deployed automatically via Continuous Delivery and Continuous Deployment [1].

This implies that these components, often running in separate containers, must communicate with each other. Furthermore, there is an interest in securing such communication links because very often confidential data is transmitted. This in turn places demands on the software development process: in order to secure (digital) communications these must be encrypted. This is also true for storing confidential data. In common cases, e.g., running a web server or storing confidential data in a database, means of authentication must be kept secret. Such means of authentication include, but are not limited to, passwords, private certificate keys, and symmetric encryption keys.

Modern software development takes place in teams whose members are in constant exchange with each other. Often, version control systems, e.g., *git* [2] are used to manage the source code and other artifacts. Also with regard to the practice of Continuous Integration (see [3]), which is a preliminary step to the aforementioned Continuous Delivery and Continuous Deployment, it is necessary to check-in *all* artifacts into the version control system. This would be grossly negligent for confidential data provided that no protective measures against unauthorized access are taken.

In this paper, we address the issue of access to an encrypted file structure in the cloud by different people in a software development team. With the Encrypted Container File (ECF), we present our own solution for a cloud-based, encrypted data storage for software development teams, in which the functionality of currently available tools is extended and their shortcomings are eliminated.

This paper is structured as follows: in Section II, there is a brief introduction to two existing solutions before the requirements are presented in Section III. In Section IV, we present an example of use and describe the structure and operations of the ECF. Following that, Section V describes implementation details. Finally, Section VI concludes the paper and gives an outlook on future work.

II. Related Work

There are different solutions to address the issue we described in Section I. In this section, we give an overview of two of these tools, *jak* and *git-crypt*, and discuss their features and shortcomings.

The tool *jak* [4] is written in Python and allows symmetric encryption of files using Advanced Encryption Standard (AES). Using the tool, one can generate keys and store them in a keyfile, which is not encrypted. To enable automatic encryption and decryption with a single command *jak* uses a special text file that contains a list of file names. This special text file can be added to the repository [4].

The practical use is limited because of sole symmetric encryption as the key distribution problem remains unsolved. Especially with growing team sizes distributing confidential data results in disproportionate effort.

Another issue with *jak* is that the confidential files' content stays unencrypted on the developers' computers. This is because *jak* decrypts these files during checkout and re-encrypts them before committing. This implies that only externals with reading access to the repository at maximum and no access to any of the developers' computers are unable to access the confidential data. A common application scenario are projects that are developed on a public repository platform.

The tool *git-crypt* [5] allows symmetric encryption of files within a *git* repository using AES, too. It shares the same limitations as *jak* in terms of access restrictions to externals.

However, *git-crypt* offers a solution to the key distribution problem by using GNU Privacy Guard (GPG) [6]. Public GPG-keys, the recipients' keys, can be added to the repository. When encrypting the confidential files within the repository *git-crypt* generates an asymmetrically encrypted keyfile for each recipient. Every recipient therefore gets access to the symmetric key and because of that is capable of decrypting the confidential files in that repository.

The tool *git-crypt* is implemented in a way that all confidential files are encrypted with the same symmetric key and this very key must therefore be shared with all recipients added to the repository. This results in coarse grained access control as there is no way to restrict access to some confidential files to a subset of the recipients. Consider the case that, e.g., secret information about the production environment should only be accessible to the production team.

Furthermore, *git-crypt* does not secure the confidential files' content on the developers' computers. This is analogous to *jak* because both tools decrypt the confidential files during checkout. The integration of *git-crypt* into the mechanisms of *git* is optional but recommended [5].

Another shortcoming of *git-crypt* is the lacking feature to remove recipients. Ayer justifies this by stating that by using a version control system a removed recipient can still access old versions of the repository and, therefore, the confidential data stored within [5]. This argument is correct as far as it goes – nevertheless, it seems sensible to implement such a mechanism into the to-be-designed ECF format since the confidential data should be updated regularly regardless. For example, certificates and passwords expire and symmetric keys should be changed regularly with regards to staff turnover.

III. Requirements Engineering

From the features and shortcomings of the *jak* and *git-crypt* tools presented in Section II, some requirements for the ECF format can be derived:

1) Mandatory encryption of confidential data,
2) possibility to modify confidential data (content is writable),
3) key distribution is no prerequisite,
4) decryption not during checkout but on demand,
5) support for multiple recipients,
6) addition and removal of recipients,
7) minimal information gain for external parties, and
8) customizable set of recipients per file.

Based on these requirements, we have decided to use the following design goals for our solution:

- Use of hybrid encryption (Items 1, 3 and 5),
- inclusion of recipient information to allow re-encryption on changes (Items 2, 5, 6 and 8),
- obfuscation of recipient information for respective external parties (Items 7 and 8), and
- delivery of the associated software as a library for embedding into existing applications (Item 4).

IV. Structure and Operations of the Encrypted Container File

This section gives an overview over the use of the ECF format in Subsection IV-A. The following subsections describe the structure of the ECF format in detail. Figure 1 shows an overview of the components of an ECF, how they are connected and related to each other. Subsection IV-B describes the general structure, components, and storage formats of an ECF. The publicly accessible fields are described in Subsection IV-C and the private fields in Subsection IV-D. The following Subsections IV-E and IV-F describe the decryption and encryption process, respectively. Finally, Subsection IV-G concludes this section with further operations that can be performed on an ECF.

A. Usage in Practice

In this subsection, we walk through the following scenario: Alice wants to encrypt a file using the ECF format and operations in such way that her friend Bob will be able to read the content, while Charlie should not be able to.

First, Alice needs access to Bob's public information, which comprises among others his public key. Bob must have created his public information beforehand. Next, Alice creates an ECF using, e.g., the CLI tool described in this paper and provided via GitHub, and adds the confidential data. After that, she can add Bob as a recipient using his public information. To retain access to the content, Alice should add herself as a recipient to the ECF. Alice can now save the ECF within a public repository and only Bob and herself are able to decrypt the file's content. Charlie, on the other hand, cannot retrieve the encryption key as he is not a recipient of that ECF and has therefore no access to the confidential data stored inside.

B. General Structure and Data Type Storage Format

Each ECF consists of three parts: A public part and two non-public/private parts. In Figure 1, the whole ECF is framed yellow, whereas the public part is colored purple. Both private parts are treated as a single datum by the symmetric encryption and are colored in blue. The following list describes the data types used in the following subsections and their storage format within an ECF:

- `Unsigned Integer`: 4 Bytes, Little Endian
- `Byte Array [x]`: x Bytes, sequential
- `String`: 4 Bytes, little endian (Length), then UTF-8 bytes without byte order mark (BOM)

The ECF format is designed to be flexible with regards to the used cipher suite. In order to allow future extensions, it allows more algorithms and cipher suites. For this paper and also for our Proof of Concept (PoC) implementation, a selection for the cipher suite was made, which is the basis for the rest of this paper:

- Key Agreement/Exchange: X25519 [7]
- Symmetric Encryption: AES-256-GCM [8]
- Signature: Ed25519 [9]
- Hash Function: SHA-512 [10]

C. Public Fields

Each ECF must provide enough information for all authorized recipients to decrypt the file. Information for encrypting, however, is not required to be public because only recipients should be able to modify the confidential data within the ECF. Hence, the public part of an ECF contains just the information required for decryption. It comprises a general part and then m identically constructed recipient-specific parts.

The general part contains the following data (in this order):

- `Container Version (Unsigned Integer)`
  ECF format version; intended for future extensions
- `Cipher Suite (Unsigned Integer)`
  Information about used algorithms
- `Public Header Length (Unsigned Integer)`
  Length of the public part in Bytes
- `Private Length (Unsigned Integer)`
  Length of the private part in Bytes
- `Recipient Count (Unsigned Integer)`
  Number of recipients in the public part (m)
- `Salt (Byte Array [16])`
  Salt value (usage described below)
- `Symmetric Nonce (Byte Array [12])`
  Symmetric nonce value (usage described below)

The first two fields, `Container Version` and `Cipher Suite`, are used to make the ECF format flexible and future-proof. However, we discuss only the cipher suite selected in Subsection IV-B.

The recipient-specific decryption information is yet to be defined. In total, m such blocks – one for each recipient – are stored after the general part. To obfuscate the number of recipients towards externals, $m \geq n$ can be chosen freely with n the true number of recipients. Random blocks, which belong to no recipient, may be inserted, which is not evident to externals. Each recipient-specific block consists of two fields: an `Identification Tag (Byte Array [16])`, which is used to assign a block to a recipient, and `Key Agreement Information` that contains recipient-specific decryption information.

The field `Identification Tag` is colored orange in Figure 1. It is the hash value truncated after 16 Bytes from the concatenation of the bit strings of the public key of the respective recipient and the `Salt` value introduced above. Shortening the hash value saves storage space and allows with $(2^8)^{16} = 2^{128}$ possible values for practically unlimited unique recipients. An authorized recipient can calculate their `Identification Tag` based on the knowledge of their own public key and the public `Salt`.

The second field, `Key Agreement Information`, contains recipient-specific information for the decryption process and is highly dependent on the used cipher suite. For the selected cipher suite, an `Ephemeral X25519 Public Key (Byte Array [32])` and an `AES Pre Key (Byte Array [32])` is stored. The first is used in the key agreement phase to obtain a second AES pre key, the latter is the first AES pre key. Subsection IV-E describes the combination

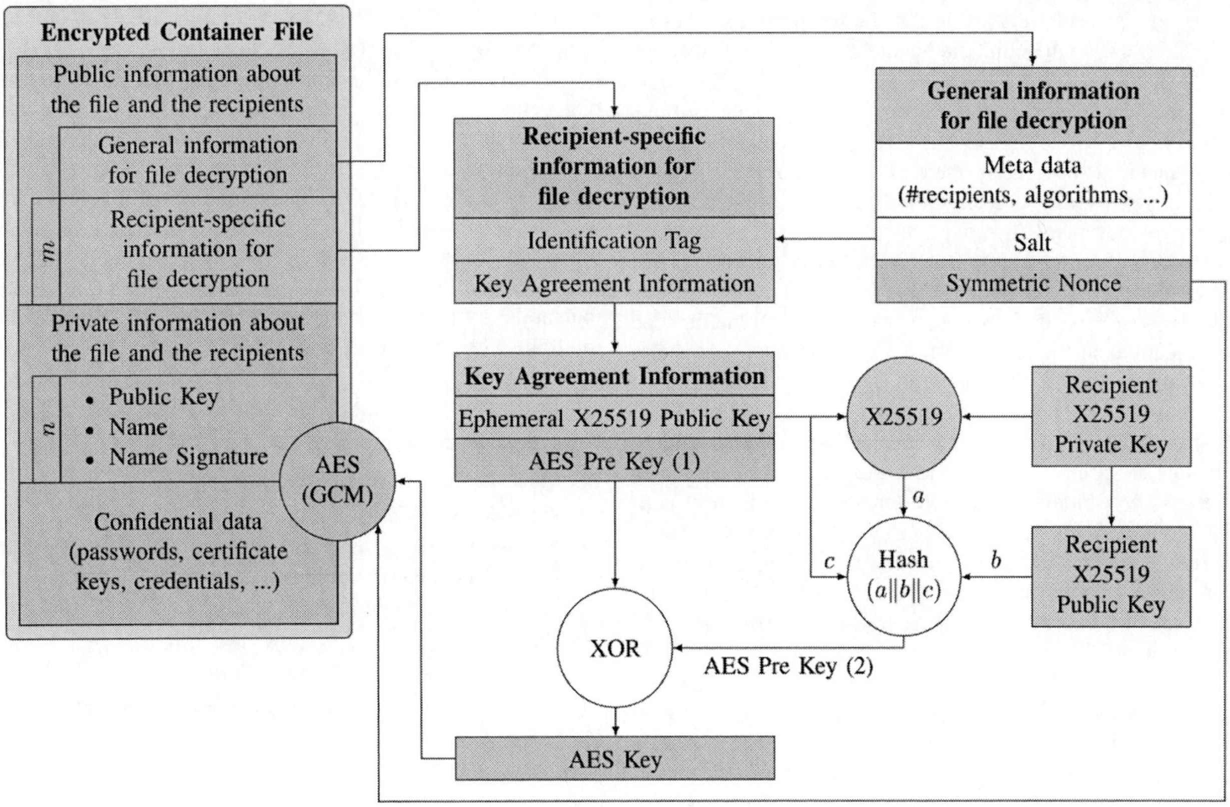

Figure 1. Diagram of the most important components of an Encrypted Container File and visualization of the interrelationships.

of the available recipient-specific information to obtain the symmetric key in more detail. The process is depicted in Figure 1 as well.

D. Private Fields

The private part of an ECF consists of two segments: First, there is information about the ECF and its recipients, and second, there is the encrypted confidential data itself. The private part is completely encrypted symmetrically and, therefore, not accessible for external parties. The following fields are stored in the private part:

- `Content Type (Unsigned Integer)`
  Describes the type of the confidential data
- `Public Header Hash (Byte Array [64])`
  Hash value of the public part
- `Recipient Count (Unsigned Integer)`
  Number of true recipients (n)
- `Recipient Information (Array [n])`
  Information about the recipients (n blocks)
- `Content Length (Unsigned Integer)`
  Length of the confidential data in Bytes (len)
- `Content (Byte Array [len])`
  Confidential data
- `Private Hash (Byte Array [64])`
  Hash value of the private part so far

The first field, `Content Type`, is intended for future use and should characterize the type of confidential data stored in `Content`. It seems reasonable that future applications using the ECF library will define and handle their own content types.

The field `Public Header Hash` contains the hash value over the whole public part of an ECF. The value for the public field `Public Header Length` (c.f. Subsection IV-C) is unknown at the time of encryption because the length of the symmetric encryption algorithm's output is not necessarily known in advance. Therefore, this field is set to the constant value of `0xECFFC0DE` (Encrypted Container File Format Code) during the calculation of the hash value. The `Public Header Hash` is used to detect unauthorized or unintended modifications of the public part, e.g., non-destructive changes of recipient-specific information of other recipients.

The fields `Recipient Count` and `Content Length` specify the number of true recipients and the length of the confidential data, respectively. The field `Recipient Information` consists of n blocks of variable length, which in turn consist of three fields: the `Public Key (Byte Array [32])` of the recipient, a `Name (String)` which contains a self-chosen name of the recipient (variable length), and the `Name Signature (Byte Array [64])` over the self-chosen name.

Every block of `Recipient Information` contains information about a recipient, so that re-encrypting the ECF is possible, e.g., after modifying confidential data. These information blocks about the recipients are stored within the private part of the ECF in order to hide them from externals. The block field `Public Key` contains the recipient's public key, which is a public Ed25519 key as specified in Subsection IV-B. One can convert an Ed25519 public key into an X25519 public key as described in [11][12]. The next block field `Name` holds a text of variable length that describes the recipient. It may contain the name of the related person or their email address. This field is for human legibility and information purposes only, e.g., when displaying the recipients or when removing existing recipients. The last block field, `Name Signature`, contains a signature over the content of `Name`. The signature is used first and foremost to ensure, that the person owing the associated private key has chosen the name, and that no changes have been made to the name by other recipients afterwards.

The field `Content` encloses the confidential data and has a theoretical limit of $2^{32} - 1$ Bytes ≈ 4 GiB. In practice, this limit should never be reached because an ECF is designed primarily to be used with passwords, certificate keys, credentials and similar confidential data.

The last field, `Private Hash`, takes the hash value over the private part up to this point. This field is inside the private part of an ECF and, therefore, the hash value is calculated before encryption. A more detailed description of the encryption process can be found in Subsection IV-F.

E. Decryption Process

This subsection describes the processes of calculating the AES key according to Figure 1. To decrypt an ECF a recipient needs both, their private X25519 key and their public Ed25519 key. Both can be calculated from the recipient's private Ed25519 key [11][12].

Nomenclature. The following notation is used: *Alice* is the recipient and $\mathrm{sk}_{\mathrm{A}}^{\mathrm{Ed}}$ denotes her private Ed25519 key, $\mathrm{pk}_{\mathrm{A}}^{\mathrm{X}}$ denotes her public X25519 key, analogously. The used cryptographic hash function is denoted by H, $a \| b$ denotes the concatenation of two bit strings a and b, and $a \oplus b$ denotes the bitwise exclusive OR (XOR) operation on two bit strings a and b of the same length. $a[0,...,n]$ denotes the truncation of the bit string a to the first n Bytes. The ephemeral public X25519 key contained in the recipient-specific decryption information is denoted by $\mathrm{pk}_{\mathrm{e}}^{\mathrm{X}}$. The function X25519$(a, B)$ describes the multiplication of scalar a with point B on the elliptic curve *Curve25519* [7].

Alice performs the following steps to obtain the AES key:

(1) Compute identification_tag $= \mathrm{H}(\mathrm{pk}_{\mathrm{A}}^{\mathrm{Ed}} \| \mathrm{Salt})[0,...,16]$.
(2) Load the decryption information $(\mathrm{pk}_{\mathrm{e}}^{\mathrm{X}}, \mathrm{k}_{\mathrm{pre1}}^{\mathrm{AES}})$ with matching identification_tag.
(3) Execute the key agreement algorithm with Alice's private X25519 key and the public ephemeral X25519 key: $\mathrm{k}_{\mathrm{shared}}^{\mathrm{X}} = \mathrm{X25519}(\mathrm{sk}_{\mathrm{A}}^{\mathrm{X}}, \mathrm{pk}_{\mathrm{e}}^{\mathrm{X}})$.
(4) Compute $\mathrm{k}_{\mathrm{pre2}}^{\mathrm{AES}} = \mathrm{H}(\mathrm{k}_{\mathrm{shared}}^{\mathrm{X}} \| \mathrm{pk}_{\mathrm{A}}^{\mathrm{X}} \| \mathrm{pk}_{\mathrm{e}}^{\mathrm{X}})[0,...,32]$.
Shortening the hash value to 32 Bytes is necessary because of the used symmetric encryption algorithm AES-256
(5) Compute $\mathrm{k}^{\mathrm{AES}} = \mathrm{k}_{\mathrm{pre1}}^{\mathrm{AES}} \oplus \mathrm{k}_{\mathrm{pre2}}^{\mathrm{AES}}$.

In Step 4 the hash function gets evaluated on the concatenation of the shared key and both public keys to obtain the second AES pre key. The reason for this is a recommendation in [13] to not use the shared key k^X_{shared} directly but to transform it with a hash function first. The question arises to why a simple hash function is used and not a Key Derivation Function (KDF). Primarily, the reason is to speed up the encryption process, because using a KDF is resource-intensive and it must be computed n times (separately for each of the n recipients). This would result in a far slower encryption process for large n. Furthermore, the input data in Step 4 is substantially longer than the symmetric pre key to be computed, which makes key stretching not required and, therefore, the use of a cryptographic hash function seems sufficient.

Finally, the private part of an ECF can be decrypted by using the computed AES key k^{AES} and the public AES nonce. In this paper, the Galois/Counter Mode (GCM) [14] was chosen for the symmetric encryption algorithm AES. Therefore, one is not required to check the authenticity of the decrypted data separately. Furthermore, instead of the field `Public Header Hash` the public part of the ECF could have been authenticated with AES-GCM. However, when supporting different modes of operation this field would have been required anyway. Hence, the field `Public Header Hash` was not removed and no additional data (*Associated Data*) was added to the AES-GCM encryption algorithm.

F. Encryption Process

The encryption process consists of an initial key and nonce generation step and an m-wise computation of the public X25519 ephemeral keys and AES pre keys. For each of the $n \leq m$ true recipients exactly one public recipient-specific decryption information block must be generated. The remaining $m - n$ blocks serve as obfuscation and may be generated using a special process as proposed in Appendix A.

Nomenclature. The same nomenclature applies as in Subsection IV-E. It gets extended by the following functions: $\text{Gen}^{AES}(256)$ and Gen^{X} denote functions to generate AES-256 keys and X25519 key pairs, respectively. $\text{RandomBytes}(x)$ denotes a function to generate a random bit string of length x Bytes.

For each recipient *Bob*, their public Ed25519 key pk^{Ed}_B is known by every recipient of that ECF because of the (private) block field `Public Key` (see Subsection IV-D). Based on pk^{Ed}_B one can calculate Bob's public X25519 key pk^X_B [11][12].

First, a symmetric AES key $k^{AES} \leftarrow \text{Gen}^{AES}(256)$, an AES nonce $\text{nonce}^{AES} \leftarrow \text{RandomBytes}(12)$ and a bit string $\text{Salt} \leftarrow \text{RandomBytes}(16)$ must be generated at random (randomness indicated by the left arrow "$\leftarrow$").

Then, the following steps are performed n times to generate the key agreement information for each recipient Bob:

(1) Compute $\text{identification\_tag} = H(pk^{Ed}_B \| \text{Salt})[0,...,16]$.
(2) Generate an ephemeral X25519 key pair: $(sk^X_e, pk^X_e) \leftarrow \text{Gen}^X$.
(3) Execute the key agreement algorithm with the private ephemeral X25519 key and Bob's public X25519 key: $k^X_{shared} = \text{X25519}(sk^X_e, pk^X_B)$.
(4) Compute $k^{AES}_{pre2} = H(k^X_{shared} \| pk^X_B \| pk^X_e)[0,...,32]$. Shortening the hash value to 32 Bytes is necessary because of the used symmetric encryption algorithm AES-256.
(5) Compute $k^{AES}_{pre1} = k^{AES} \oplus k^{AES}_{pre2}$.

Steps 2 and 3 correspond to a "half" Diffie-Hellman key exchange [15] that gets completed during decryption (see Subsection IV-E) in Step 3.

For each recipient Bob the recipient-specific information can be written into the public part of the ECF. This information per recipient consists of identification_tag, public ephemeral X25519 key pk^X_e and AES pre key k^{AES}_{pre1}.

The values Salt and nonce^{AES} are valid for all recipients and are written into their respective fields (see Subsection IV-C).

G. Further ECF Operations

This subsection introduces more ECF operations which are based on the elementary operations Decryption (Subsection IV-E) and Encryption (Subsection IV-F). The same nomenclature is used as in the specified subsections. It gets extended by the function $\text{Dec}^{ECF}(sk^{Ed}_A, \mathcal{E})$ which denotes the decryption of an ECF $\mathcal{E}$ with Alice's private Ed25519 key sk^{Ed}_A. This function returns a tuple (R, p) after successful decryption, with R being the set of all n recipients $R = \{r_1, r_2, \ldots, r_n\}$ and p being the bit string of the decrypted confidential data. Analogous to this, the function $\text{Enc}^{ECF}(R, p)$ encrypts the confidential data p for the recipients R and returns an ECF $\mathcal{E}$.

1) Modification of Confidential Data:

Let $p' = \text{modify}(p)$ be the new bit string created by modification of the original confidential data p. The replacement of the confidential data within an ECF $\mathcal{E}$ is done by these steps:

(1) $(R, p) = \text{Dec}^{ECF}(sk^{Ed}_A, \mathcal{E})$
(2) $p' = \text{modify}(p)$
(3) $\mathcal{E}' \leftarrow \text{Enc}^{ECF}(R, p')$

2) Addition of a New Recipient:

Recipient Alice wants to add a new recipient Bob to an existing ECF. Bob's public Ed25519 key is denoted by pk^{Ed}_B, the bit string of his name by name_B. The signature over Bob's name is denoted by $s = \text{signature}^{Ed}(sk^{Ed}_B, \text{name}_B)$. Alice performs the following steps to add Bob to the recipient list:

(1) Alice verifies the Signature s: $\text{verify}^{Ed}(s, pk^{Ed}_B) \stackrel{?}{=} \textit{Valid}$.
(2) If the signature is invalid, abort the operation, if the signature is valid, proceed.
(3) $r_B = (pk^{Ed}_B, \text{name}_B, s)$
(4) $(R, p) = \text{Dec}^{ECF}(sk^{Ed}_A, \mathcal{E})$
(5) Alice checks whether Bob is already in the recipient list: $R \cap \{r_B\} \stackrel{?}{=} \emptyset$ (Compare Ed25519 public keys).
(6) If Bob is already a recipient, abort the operation, if Bob is not a recipient, proceed.
(7) Optionally, Alice can check if name_B already exists in one r_i and abort the operation if necessary.
(8) $R' = R \cup \{r_B\} = \{r_1, r_2, \ldots, r_n, r_B\}$

(9) $\mathcal{E}' \leftarrow \text{Enc}^{\text{ECF}}(R', p)$

3) Removal of a Recipient:

Recipient Alice wants to remove a recipient Bob from an existing ECF. Bob's public Ed25519 key $\text{pk}_\text{B}^\text{Ed}$ and/or the bit string of his name name_B must be known. If only his name is known, it must be unique within the ECF $\mathcal{E}$. Alice performs the following steps to remove Bob from the recipient list:

(1) $(R, p) = \text{Dec}^{\text{ECF}}(\text{sk}_\text{A}^\text{Ed}, \mathcal{E})$
(2) Alice searches for r_B in R based on his public key $\text{pk}_\text{B}^\text{Ed}$ or his name name_B.
(3) If r_B does not exist (Bob is not a recipient of $\mathcal{E}$), abort the operation, if r_B exists proceed.
(4) $R' = R \setminus \{r_\text{B}\}$
(5) $\mathcal{E}' \leftarrow \text{Enc}^{\text{ECF}}(R', p)$

When removing recipients, one does not require any private keys during the encryption process. This implies that recipients of an ECF can remove themselves. It is therefore the task of the implementation to warn the user or abort the operation if the user attempts to do this. Additionally, the implementation should also realize additional security functions if, for example, only the creator of the confidential data stored in an ECF is allowed to add or remove recipients. Finally, it must be noted that the restriction explained in Section II is still true: Former recipients are still able to access old versions of an ECF when using a version control system.

V. Implementation Details

A PoC was implemented using *C#* and the *.NET 6.0* runtime. All cryptographic primitives were provided by the portable library *Sodium* [16], which is a fork of the *NaCl* [17] library. To use *Sodium* with *.NET* a wrapper is needed. For this PoC the wrapper library *NSec* [18] was used.

A. Implementation of ECF Functionality

The implementation in *C#* was subdivided into two projects: `ECF.Core` and `ECF.CLI`. The `ECF.Core` project contains all functionality of the ECF and helps with managing private keys (see Subsection V-B). `ECF.Core` is a library and can be included into other projects (according to requirements in Section III). It is used by the `ECF.CLI` project which provides a command line interface to the ECF functionality.

The `Create(CipherSuite, ContentType)` function in class `EncryptedContainer` implements the ECF creation process using the given cipher suite and content type. For this PoC the aforementioned cipher suite (see Subsection IV-B) is implemented as well as a single content type: *BLOB*. Because of the GCM mode of operation, the execution platform must support the instruction set extension *AES-NI*. As a rule, this can only lead to problems when using very old processors or virtual machines.

An object of type `EncryptedContainer` can be encrypted using the function `Write(Stream)`. The output is written into the parameter `Stream`. Analogously, one can obtain an unencrypted object of this type using the class function `Load(Stream, ECFKey)`. It is necessary to provide a private Ed25519 key of a recipient to that function. Per default all name's signatures are verified. This can be disabled to achieve better runtime performance during decryption. The property `ContentStream` of an `EncryptedContainer` object provides read and write access to the confidential data.

To protect the private key and the confidential data the implementation uses protected memory spaces, if possible. The library *Sodium* provides suitable functions for this [19], which in turn are used by *NSec*. Furthermore, heap allocations are replaced by stack allocations wherever possible using the *C#* keyword `stackalloc` [20]. Alternatively, when using memory that cannot be protected via *Sodium* or stack allocation, the implementation pins these memory regions in memory to prevent the Garbage Collector from arbitrarily copying them. Furthermore, used memory regions are actively deleted before they are freed.

B. Private Key Management

Using ECFs requires private keys that should never be stored unencrypted. Therefore, the `ECF.Core` project uses AES-256 (GCM) to encrypt the private keys. The encryption key is derived from a user-provided password using Argon2id [21][22]. Argon2id aims to enforce costly calculations that cannot be parallelized or otherwise shortened (in time) by an attacker. The algorithm can be configured arbitrarily in order to keep the required computing time variable. For the PoC implementation the following settings were chosen:

- Degree of parallelism: 1 (Limit by *Sodium*)
- Memory requirements: 2 GiB
- Number of iterations: 5

This results in an approximate run time of 5 s on an *Intel Core i5-6600K* with newer processors being presumably faster.

The private key is needed when decrypting an ECF and when creating an ECF. For the latter it is necessary to add oneself as a recipient to that ECF, which includes signing the name. Therefore, `ECF.CLI` always prompts the user's password to load the encrypted private key.

VI. Conclusion and Future Work

In this paper we introduced Encrypted Container File, a hybrid-encrypted multi-recipient file structure aimed to store confidential data and share it with a customizable set of recipients. Full examples of basic and advanced operations recipients can perform on an ECF were presented in this paper. Although we were using a single cipher suite as described in Subsection IV-B, the file format supports multiple cipher suites which can be implemented analogously. The PoC implementation demonstrates this by implementing both SHA-512 and SHA-256 as cryptographic hash functions resulting in two different cipher suites.

The full code of the PoC implementation and unit tests for that code are available at:

https://github.com/Hirnmoder/ECF

For the future, we plan to add additional cipher suites to ECF. Additional functionalities are also possible depending on the feedback we get from the community.

REFERENCES

[1] Intellectsoft. "Top 8 software development trends in 2022," Intellectsoft. (Dec. 3, 2021), [Online]. Available: https://www.intellectsoft.net/blog/software-development-trends/ (visited on 06/05/2023).

[2] Git. "Git." (2023), [Online]. Available: https://git-scm.com/ (visited on 06/05/2023).

[3] M. Fowler. "Continuous integration." (May 1, 2006), [Online]. Available: https://www.martinfowler.com/articles/continuousIntegration.html (visited on 06/05/2023).

[4] Dispel LLC. "Jak – simple git encryption," Dispel LLC. (2017), [Online]. Available: https://jak.readthedocs.io/en/latest/ (visited on 06/05/2023).

[5] A. Ayer. "Git-crypt – transparent file encryption in git." (2023), [Online]. Available: https://www.agwa.name/projects/git-crypt/ (visited on 06/05/2023).

[6] W. Koch, N. Ellmenreich, M. Ashley, *et al.* "The gnu privacy guard," The GnuPG Project. (May 31, 2023), [Online]. Available: https://gnupg.org/ (visited on 06/05/2023).

[7] D. J. Bernstein, "Curve25519: New diffie-hellman speed records," in *Public Key Cryptography - PKC 2006*, Springer Berlin Heidelberg, 2006, pp. 207–228.

[8] D. A. McGrew and J. Viega. "The galois/counter mode of operation (GCM)," National Institute of Standards and Technology. (May 31, 2005), [Online]. Available: https://csrc.nist.rip/groups/ST/toolkit/BCM/documents/proposedmodes/gcm/gcm-revised-spec.pdf (visited on 06/05/2023).

[9] D. J. Bernstein, N. Duif, T. Lange, P. Schwabe, and B.-Y. Yang, "High-speed high-security signatures," *Journal of Cryptographic Engineering*, vol. 2, no. 2, pp. 77–89, Aug. 2012.

[10] Q. H. Dang, "Secure hash standard," Tech. Rep., Jul. 2015. DOI: 10.6028/nist.fips.180-4. [Online]. Available: https://doi.org/10.6028/nist.fips.180-4.

[11] "Squeamish Ossifrage". "Curve25519 over Ed25519 for key exchange? Why?" Crypto Stack Exchange. (Mar. 19, 2019), [Online]. Available: https://crypto.stackexchange.com/a/68129 (visited on 06/05/2023).

[12] The Sodium Authors. "Ed25519 to curve25519 – libsodium." (2023), [Online]. Available: https://doc.libsodium.org/advanced/ed25519-curve25519 (visited on 06/05/2023).

[13] The Sodium Authors. "Point*scalar multiplication – libsodium." (2021), [Online]. Available: https://doc.libsodium.org/advanced/scalar_multiplication (visited on 06/05/2023).

[14] M. J. Dworkin, "Recommendation for block cipher modes of operation: Galois/counter mode (gcm) and gmac," Tech. Rep., 2007. DOI: 10.6028/nist.sp.800-38d. [Online]. Available: https://doi.org/10.6028/nist.sp.800-38d.

[15] W. Diffie and M. E. Hellman, "New directions in cryptography," *IEEE Transactions on Information Theory*, vol. 22, no. 6, pp. 644–654, Nov. 1976.

[16] The Sodium Authors. "Introduction – libsodium." (2022), [Online]. Available: https://doc.libsodium.org/ (visited on 06/05/2023).

[17] D. J. Bernstein, T. Lange, and P. Schwabe. "Nacl: Networking and cryptography library." (Mar. 15, 2016), [Online]. Available: https://nacl.cr.yp.to (visited on 06/05/2023).

[18] K. Hartke. "Nsec – modern cryptography for .net core." (2022), [Online]. Available: https://nsec.rocks/ (visited on 06/05/2023).

[19] The Sodium Authors. "Secure memory." (2022), [Online]. Available: https://doc.libsodium.org/memory_management (visited on 06/05/2023).

[20] Microsoft Docs. "stackalloc expression (c# reference)," Microsoft. (Apr. 12, 2023), [Online]. Available: https://docs.microsoft.com/en-us/dotnet/csharp/language-reference/operators/stackalloc (visited on 06/05/2023).

[21] A. Biryukov, D. Dinu, and D. Khovratovich. "Argon2: The memory-hard function for password hashing and other applications." version 1.3. (Mar. 24, 2017), [Online]. Available: https://raw.githubusercontent.com/P-H-C/phc-winner-argon2/master/argon2-specs.pdf (visited on 06/05/2023).

[22] The Sodium Authors. "The pwhash* api." (2022), [Online]. Available: https://doc.libsodium.org/password_hashing/default_phf (visited on 06/05/2023).

[23] "fgrieu". "Using sha2 as random number generator?" Crypto Stack Exchange. (Jun. 20, 2020), [Online]. Available: https://crypto.stackexchange.com/a/81459 (visited on 06/05/2023).

APPENDIX

A. Generating $m - n$ Obfuscation Blocks

In Subsection IV-F the generation process for the n public recipient-specific blocks was described. The remaining $m-n$ blocks serve as obfuscation blocks to hide the true number of recipients to externals. These obfuscation blocks should not be random bit strings because there is a possibility that the outputs of the used algorithms are subject to statistical effects. This would allow an external party to distinguish between real blocks and obfuscation blocks and therefore determine n.

To avoid this, we suggest that the $m - n$ obfuscation blocks are constructed using randomly generated Ed25519 and X25519 key pairs. The function $\mathrm{Gen}^{\mathrm{Ed}}$ denotes the creation of an Ed25519 key pair and the function $\mathrm{Convert}^{\mathrm{X}}(\mathrm{sk}^{\mathrm{Ed}})$ converts an Ed25519 private key into an X25519 key pair. The following steps are performed for each obfuscation block:

(1) Generate a random key pair:
$(\mathrm{sk}_\mathrm{r}^{\mathrm{Ed}}, \mathrm{pk}_\mathrm{r}^{\mathrm{Ed}}) \leftarrow \mathrm{Gen}^{\mathrm{Ed}}, \quad (\mathrm{sk}_\mathrm{r}^{\mathrm{X}}, \mathrm{pk}_\mathrm{r}^{\mathrm{X}}) = \mathrm{Convert}^{\mathrm{X}}(\mathrm{sk}_\mathrm{r}^{\mathrm{Ed}})$.

(2) Compute $\mathrm{identification\_tag} = \mathrm{H}(\mathrm{pk}_\mathrm{r}^{\mathrm{Ed}} \| \mathrm{Salt})[0,\ldots,16]$.

(3) Generate an ephemeral X25519 key pair:
$(\mathrm{sk}_\mathrm{e}^{\mathrm{X}}, \mathrm{pk}_\mathrm{e}^{\mathrm{X}}) \leftarrow \mathrm{Gen}^{\mathrm{X}}$.

(4) Generate a random AES-256 key:
$\mathrm{k}_\mathrm{r}^{\mathrm{AES}} \leftarrow \mathrm{Gen}^{\mathrm{AES}}(256)$ or $\mathrm{k}_\mathrm{r}^{\mathrm{AES}} \leftarrow \mathrm{RandomBytes}(32)$.

(5) Execute the key agreement algorithm with the private ephemeral and the random public X25519 keys:
$\mathrm{k}_{\mathrm{shared}}^{\mathrm{X}} = \mathrm{X25519}(\mathrm{sk}_\mathrm{e}^{\mathrm{X}}, \mathrm{pk}_\mathrm{r}^{\mathrm{X}})$.

(6) Compute $\mathrm{k}_{\mathrm{pre2}}^{\mathrm{AES}} = \mathrm{H}(\mathrm{k}_{\mathrm{shared}}^{\mathrm{X}} \| \mathrm{pk}_\mathrm{r}^{\mathrm{X}} \| \mathrm{pk}_\mathrm{e}^{\mathrm{X}})[0,\ldots,32]$.
Shortening the hash value to 32 Bytes is necessary because of the used symmetric encryption algorithm AES-256.

(7) Compute $\mathrm{k}_{\mathrm{pre1}}^{\mathrm{AES}} = \mathrm{k}_\mathrm{r}^{\mathrm{AES}} \oplus \mathrm{k}_{\mathrm{pre2}}^{\mathrm{AES}}$.

Provided that the used cryptographic hash function generates truly random looking bit strings, on can simplify the generation process to increase runtime performance. The assumption of true random looking bit strings is justified with the input lengths used in Subsections IV-E and IV-F, see [23].

(1) Generate an ephemeral X25519 key pair:
$(\mathrm{sk}_\mathrm{e}^{\mathrm{X}}, \mathrm{pk}_\mathrm{e}^{\mathrm{X}}) \leftarrow \mathrm{Gen}^{\mathrm{X}}$.

(2) Generate $\mathrm{identification\_tag} \leftarrow \mathrm{RandomBytes}(16)$.

(3) Generate $\mathrm{k}_{\mathrm{pre1}}^{\mathrm{AES}} \leftarrow \mathrm{RandomBytes}(32)$.

The shortened generation process is used in the PoC implementation. The number m is randomly chosen in dependence on n, such that $\max\{8, 2n\} \geq m \geq n$.

Generation of Distributed Denial of Service Network Data with Phyton and Scapy

Stefan Görtz
Computer Science and Mathematics
Ostbayerische Technische Hochschule
Regensburg, Germany
email:
stefan1.goertz@st.oth-regensburg.de

Sebastian Fischer
Computer Science and Mathematics
Ostbayerische Technische Hochschule
Regensburg, Germany
email:
sebastian.fischer@oth-regensburg.de

Rudolf Hackenberg
Computer Science and Mathematics
Ostbayerische Technische Hochschule
Regensburg, Germany
email:
rudolf.hackenberg@oth-regensburg.de

***Abstract*—Distributed Denial of Service attacks are among the most common and widespread network attacks. Due to their nature, they are difficult to defend. Intrusion detection systems, based on machine learning, are a promising approach to counter this threat. But to train these systems, data sets with Distributed Denial of Service attacks are needed. An implemented Python program, which creates Denial of Services packets and simulates distributed sending by multithreading, is presented. Unlike synthetically generated data with the use of simulators, real network traffic is generated. This eliminates errors and offers a better basis of data, as machine learning algorithms need data that is as error-free as possible in order to learn efficiently.**

***Keywords*—DDoS; Scapy; Synflood; Udpflood; PCAP; IDS.**

I. Introduction

Distributed Denial of Service (DDoS) attacks are among the most common network-based attacks and cause major economic damage. In the third quarter of 2022, the number of DDoS attacks increased sharply by 90%, compared to the third quarter of the previous year [1]. Internet of Things (IoT) devices are particularly vulnerable to these attacks, as they are accessible via the Internet and usually exchange data with cloud servers.

Detecting DDoS attacks is difficult, because the attack packets are indistinguishable from ordinary network traffic [2] and the packages come from many different sources. An intrusion detection system (IDS) is usually used to detect these attacks. However, conventional IDSs are no longer sufficient for more sophisticated attacks. The use of an artificial intelligence-based intrusion detection system (iIDS) is a promising approach to detect DDoS attacks. But for the development of an iIDS, attack data is needed to train the iIDS' machine learning modules. Since real data is not easily available and not classified, generated data is mostly used. Therefore, this paper presents an approach to generate real training data using Python and Scapy. It aims at a possible solution to the following question: How can DDoS network data on IoT devices suitable for machine learning be generated?

The paper is structured as follows: in section 2, the related work is introduced, in section 3 the theoretical foundations are shown, then our methods are presented in section 4 and the results are shown in section 5. Section 6 contains the discussion of the results. Subsequently, in section 7, we draw a conclusion and in the end in section 8, an outlook is given.

II. Related Work

Singh et al. [3] use the network simulation software NS2 to generate a network of 8 clients. They generate network traces of attack data, which consists injected packets, mixed with an attack based on a DDoS dataset. Through this dataset, a DDoS attack of 130 attack hosts on one target is generated for the duration of 50 seconds with a maximum throughput rate of 90,000 bps.

Arora and Dalal [4] use NET stress, a network stressing tool to introduce DDoS Attacks. They generate TCP, as well as UDP connections and carry out UDP flood and IGMP Flood attacks for the duration of 50 secs and 38 secs while benchmarking the network performance.

Baly et al. [5] use the graphical networksimulator GNS3 to create a topology of a webserver, three computers and one intruder with a Kali Linux distribution. The intruder carrys out DDoS attacks, captured by wireshark as pcap files.

Alzahrani and Hong [6] use the OMNET++ network simulator to generate DDoS attack network traffic in a simulated cloud environment. They generate various DDoS scenarios: Synflooding, HTTP flooding and UDP flooding. In addition, they generate non-intrusive traffic.

In contrast to the synthetically generated network traffic, with the use of simulators, we generate real network traffic. Generating network data synthetically has some potential sources of error. These are eliminated by performing the DDoS attacks in a real network environment. Furthermore, we can conduct attacks with longer durations and more individual attack hosts.

III. Theoretical Foundations

This section lays the theoretical introduction for DDoS data generation with Python using our method.

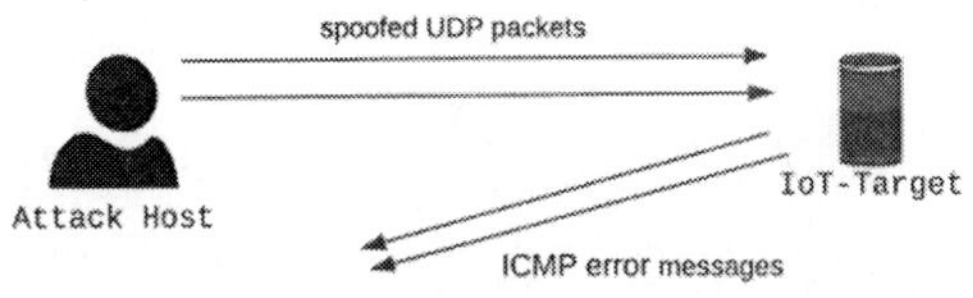

Fig. 1. UDP flooding

A. Denial of Service

Denial of Service (DoS) attacks aim to make a service unavailable, that is accessible via the Internet, unusable for legitimate visitors [7]. A distinction is made between two different attack categories, on the one hand attackers can aim to overload the network and hardware resources, for example bandwidth, memory and CPU cycles of the target, on the other hand, the behavior of the network protocols used, for example TCP or UDP, can be abused [8]. In the case of a successful attack, the entire resources of the attack target or protocol instance are consumed by the attacker and legitimate requests can no longer be processed [9].

B. Distributed Denial of Service

DDoS attacks use the DoS techniques with the help of many attack hosts. The attack hosts are devices, accessible through the Internet, which are infected with malicious code and involuntarily participate in the network attacks [8].

C. Anatomy of DDoS Attacks

Most DDoS attacks (64% in 2022) exploit the Transmission Control Protocol (TCP), followed by the User Datagram Protocol (UDP) with 22% [10]. The motivation of most DDoS attacks is political or economic. In so-called ransom DDoS attacks, cybercriminals blackmail their target into paying a ransom or holding out the prospect of a DDoS attack. The most commonly targeted industry segments include the aviation industry, government institutions, telecom facilities and media houses. The most frequent attacks occurred at intervals of ten to twenty minutes, followed by attacks lasting one to three hours [11].

D. UDP Flooding

UDP defines a minimal network protocol for connectionless data transfer with no guarantee of complete and correct data transfer. Applications create an UDP header for their data and transfer it via Internet Protocol (IP).

This DDoS attack variant uses a large number of packets to exhaust the hardware resources of the recipient. Accordingly, UDP flooding attacks belong to the first DDoS category. To carry out the attack, a high volume of UDP packets with spoofed IP address is sent to random ports of the target. UDP implementation on the receiver side searches for the corresponding application that accepts UDP packets on the addressed port. If no application is found, it responds with an Internet Control Message Protocol (ICMP) error message [12]. Figure 1 depicts the sequence of an UDP flooding attack. By permanently addressing different ports, it is ensured that the recipient sends such ICMP error messages. The attack is successful when the volume of malicious packets is such that the victim's bandwidth is consumed and legitimate requests cannot be answered.

E. SYN Flooding

Besides UDP flooding attacks, synchronize (SYN) flooding attacks are the most common type of attack. They exploit TCP, and thus belong to the second category of DDoS attacks. TCP provides reliable, bilateral data transmission between two network-enabled applications. Data is transmitted as TCP segments over the IP. Checksums and the division of data into sequences ensure a complete and error-free transmission. As in the event of an error, individual TCP segments are sent again [13].

A TCP connection is described by two sockets and is uniquely identifiable by its parameters: **socket 1** *source IP address*, *source port* and **socket 2** *destination IP address* and *destination port*. The data to be sent is divided into TCP segments, each of which is assigned a sequence number, to ensure correct data transmission. For this purpose, the window size is defined within the TCP header as a set of data, after which the recipient checks it for completeness and acknowledges it. In addition, various control bits can be set as flags, for example, for the establishment or termination of the connection [13].

Connection setup: A TCP instance with no active connection is in the *LISTEN* state, while waiting for incoming connections. The connection between two TCP instances is established by a *3-way-handshake* (see Figure 2), to synchronize the sequence numbers [13][14]:

1) Host A sends a packet with a random inital sequence number x and the SYN flag set.
2) Host B responds with a set SYN and ACK flag, acknowledges the sequence number of the first message ACK number = $x+1$ and its own random inital sequence number y. A half-open connection now exists. The state of the connection changes on the receiving host from *LISTEN* to *SYN-RECEIVED.*
3) Host A acknowledges the message from Host B with ACK number = $y + 1$ and set ACK flag. The connection between the two hosts is now active and has the state *ESTABLISHED.*

SYN flooding is a DoS attack on a host with a TCP instance. The goal of the attack is to create so many half-open TCP connections on the attacked host that no more legitimate requests can be accepted. For each incoming

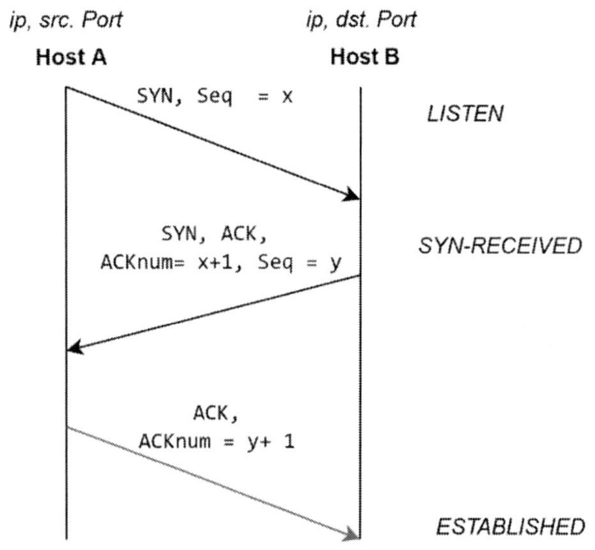

Fig. 2. TCP 3-way-handshake

attacker connection request, a TCP connection must be stored in the backlog queue with its state. The attacker's goal is to overflow this storage structure and prevent legitimate connections from being accepted. To perform the attack, a host opens a TCP connection by sending a synchronize packet. The destination responds with a SYN-ACK packet.

The state of the connection changes from *LISTEN* to *SYN-RECEIVED*. These connections are stored in the backlog, where the connections dwell until the sender acknowledges the receiver's response or the SYN-RECEIVED timer expires. But as the attack hosts are spoofed, they never acknowledge the connection. The attacker is aiming to completely block the backlog. The TCP standard does not define a universal approach for a full backlog. Common implementations now ignore new requests or remove the oldest requests from the backlog. However, an attacker with enough resources can still continuously overfill the backlog.

IV. Methods

To generate the DDoS network traffic, a Python program was implemented that uses the Scapy library, to create network packets. Using Scapy, the packet parameters can be set individually. This allows spoofing of the source IP and source Media-Access-Control (MAC) address. In addition, network packets of different protocols can be generated, to realize the two DoS attacks described above. UDP packets on the one hand, and TCP packets with the SYN flag set, on the other hand.

A. Test Setup

To generate the DDoS network data, a test environment (see Figure 3) was installed with a selection of different IoT devices as attack targets: Amazon Echo 2 and smart cameras from the manufacturers Antela, Nedis, SV3C and Tapo.

These devices are located in a Wi-Fi network created by an Unifi Access Point nanoHD. The Wi-Fi network is integrated into the network created by an Ubiquiti Edge Router via an Unifi Switch Flex Mini. The IoT devices gain access to the Internet via this router.

To record the data traffic, a tcpdump instance runs on the Unifi Access Point nanoHD. This instance intercepts the Wi-Fi internal data traffic via its network interface. The tcpdump recording runs continuously to capture both, normal network traffic from the IoT devices, and attack traffic. To perform attacks on the IoT devices, the attacker connects to the Ubiquiti router.

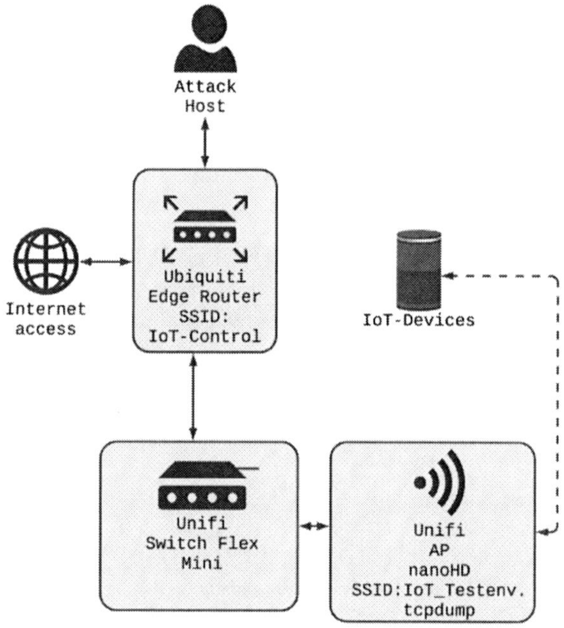

Fig. 3. Network diagram of the test environment

B. Implemented Python Program

The objectdiagram of the implemented Python DDoS data generation program can be seen in Figure 4. DDoS attacks are carried out in two stages. In the first stage, the attack is planned. Either manually or randomly generated attacks are planned automatically, for which an attack planner class has been written. In both cases, a target is selected from the IoT test setup, then an attack protocol, either synflooding or updflooding is selected. Next, the attack host network is planned. Each host is identified by a combination of a spoofed IP address, as well as a spoofed MAC address. The number of hosts and the number of packets, to be sent per host, is specified. The planned attack is written to a comma-separated values

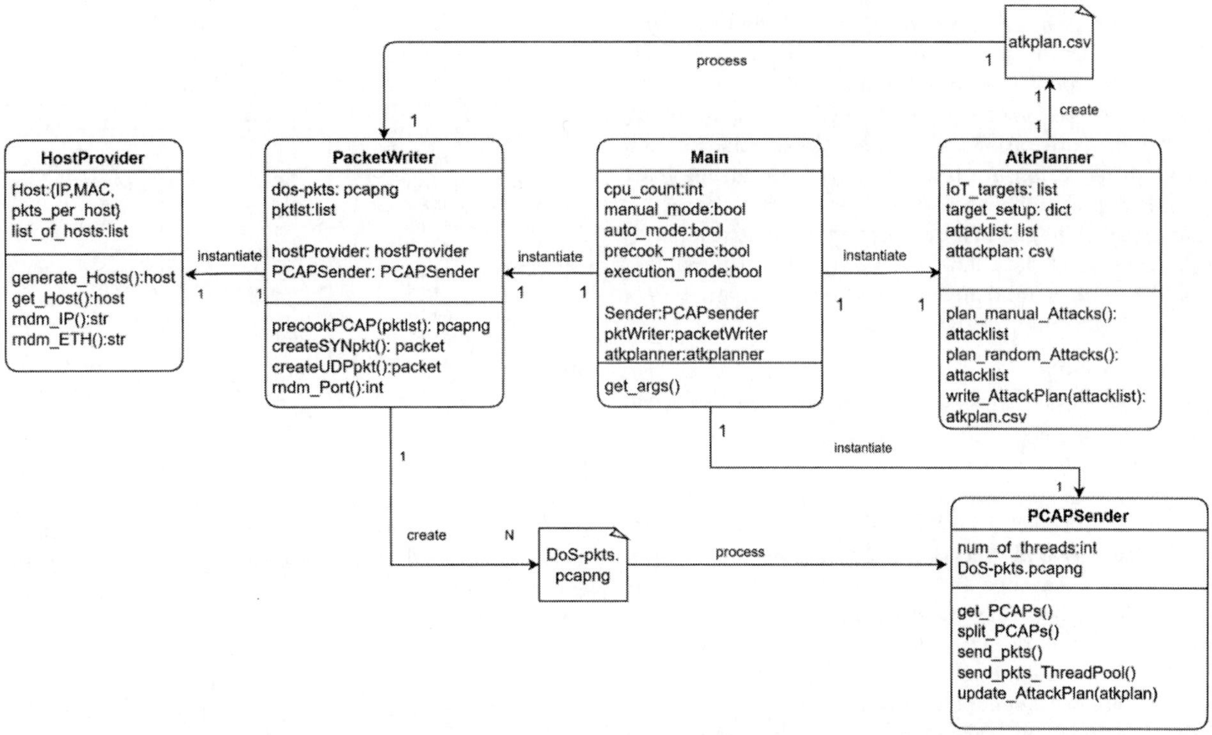

Fig. 4. Objectdiagram of the implemented Python DDoS data generation program

file that serves as persistent storage. After the attack planning is completed, the attack packets are created by a `PacketWriter` class with the help of Scapy and written to a pcapng file.

In the second stage, the actual attack is carried out by the `pcapsender` class. The previously created pcapng files are read into the Random Access Memory (RAM) by Scapy. A threadpool is created depending on the cpu count of the attacker PC. The read packets are divided into chunks for parallelized transmission, depending on the number of cpu cores used. Afterward, the packet chunks are passed to `tcpreplay` by Scapy and processed in parallel.

C. Packet design

On ISO OSI Layer 2, both packet types have a spoofed MAC address. In ISO OSI layer 3, both types of packets contain a spoofed IP address which ensures that no IP addresses from private areas are used. Additionally, this layer contains the destination address of the attack target. ISO OSI Layer 4 is individually designed according to the attack protocol and contains either the UDP or TCP header.

The depicted Python function (see Figure 5) of the `PacketWriter` class takes a host dictionary from the previously created host network, the attack target IP address and its TCP port as parameters. A TCP packet is generated from the transferred data, the spoofed sending

```
def createSYNpacket(self, host,
    target_IP, target_PORT):

     src_MAC = host.get("src_MAC")
     src_IP = host.get("src_IP")
     src_PORT = host.get("src_PORT")

     seqN = random.randint(0, 65535)
     rndm_raw = random.randint(1,1453)
     payload = Raw(b'SYNFLOOD' + b'X'*rndm_raw)

     packet = Ether(src=src_MAC)
     / IP(dst=target_IP, src=src_IP) \
     / TCP(sport=src_PORT, dport=target_PORT,
     flags="S", seq=seqN, window=0)\
     / payload

    return packet
```

Fig. 5. Python function for TCP synchronize packet creation

parameters are taken from fields of the `host dictionary`. A random sequence number is generated for the TCP header. The payload receives a binary coded flag and is provided with a random payload length to increase the variance. Finally, the synchronize flag is set and the window number is defined with 0. The package is assembled layer by layer through Scapy and returned to a packet list.

Analogous to the `createSYNpacket` function (see Figure 5), the Python function `createUDPpacket` creates UDP packets. The spoofed sending parameters are taken from a passed `host dictionary`. The sending port is randomly assigned for more variance. Likewise, the destination port is randomized to ensure that most packets do not reach an UDP application by chance. The payload contains a binary encoded flag to mark the packet as an attack packet in the context of data labeling. In addition, the payload is padded with a random length of binary characters to increase the variance of the packets.

D. Packet sending

For sending, Scapy passes the prepared packages to the `tcpreplay` instance, installed on the attack computer. This creates a temporary pcapng file. This process is the bottleneck of the program, besides the number of threads. However, a loop factor can be defined, so that the same packet is sent several times. This can increase the speed, at the expense of variance. In the case of UDP flooding, this is less serious, since only the payload length represents an increase in the data set. Whereas with the synchronize packets of a synflooding attack, additionally, the same sequence number is sent. This accumulation can also occur in DDoS attacks by real botnets, depending on how the flooding function is implemented. If the loop factor is used, the packet transmission rate increases continuously, since the packets which are read from the temporary pcap file can be stored in the RAM.

E. Data Processing

The records created by tcpdump are exported and processed at cyclic intervals. The network data set can thus be continuously expanded. These pcaps are then read and processed by another Python program. Attack packets are marked as such and labeled with the type of DDoS attack that the data set is suitable for supervised learning procedures. The Python library Scapy is also used for this purpose; its rdpcap function reads in the recorded packets and converts them afterwards into Python dictionaries. Each dictionary is extended by the fields intrusion (boolean) and attacktype (string, *SYN-FLOOD* or *UDPFLOOD*), this implementation allows an easy extension with further attack variants in the future. For each packet, it is checked, if the payload contains an intrusion flag. If the test is positive, the intrusion flag is set and the attacktype is noted. If the test is negative, the intrusion flag is set to false and the attacktype is set to none. Optionally, the intrusion flag can be removed from the payload. Otherwise, the payload should not be used for evaluation by machine learning. Finally, the now labeled package dictionaries are inserted into a SQL database for further use.

V. Results

This section describes the results of the generated DDoS data by the implemented Python program. It generates DDoS attack data of the two most common DDoS variants. Continuous data logging in the test environment generates records of idle network traffic intermingled with the network traffic of DDoS attacks. As a result, the records also contain the beginning and ending of the attacks. This is important to train machine learning applications on attack detections.

TABLE I
DDoS attack effects on IoT devices

DDoS effects on IoT Devices		
IoT device	**Attack type**	**Effect**
Amazon Echo	synflood	success
Amazon Echo	udpflood	no success
Nedis Cam Gray	synflood	success
Nedis Cam Gray	udpflood	success
Tapo Cam C100	synflood	success
Tapo Cam C100	udpflood	success
Antela Speed Cam	synflood	success
Antela Speed Cam	udpflood	no success
Nedis cam white	synflood	success
Nedis cam white	udpflood	no success
SV3C camera	synflood	success
SV3C camera	udpflood	no success

The following impact of the attacks on the IoT devices could be observed. The SYN flooding attacks were successful in every case. The devices were unreachable within a few seconds up to a maximum of 60 seconds, for the duration of the attack. Table I depicts the measured effects of the DDoS attacks on the IoT devices.

UDP flooding attacks did not cause every device to fail. This is probably because the IoT devices do not process incoming UDP packets, they ignore them and therefore do not allocate resources.

VI. Discussion

This section discusses the research question defined at the outset. To generate realistic DDoS network data, the attacks carried out must mimic real DDoS botnets. An adequately large host network must be simulated for this purpose. Each of these hosts has an individual combination of spoofed IP and MAC addresses. This means that the network traffic reflects a large number of senders, even though the packets are sent from the same attacking host. This ensures a high variance in the data captured.

The following points address the requirements for the generated data:

1) Packets: Care is taken during packet generation to ensure that valid packets are generated for the protocol in question. This is ensured by evaluating the tcpdump captures. Malformed packets can be detected and corresponding errors have to be fixed, to generate a record of real network traffic.
2) Distribution: To simulate not only DoS attacks, multiple packets are sent simultaneously by using parallelization with threads.

3) Attack duration: Various attack scenarios are simulated. The attack duration takes place in intervals ranging from ten minutes to several hours. Weighing whether to maximize the attack quantity or to follow the parameters as described in the section Anatomy of DDoS Attacks.
4) Non attack traffic: In order to generate qualitative datasets, it is important that the network recordings do not only consist of attacks. So, idle communication of the IoT devices is also recorded.

VII. Conclusion

Finally, we evaluate the advantages and limitations of generating DDoS attack data with the implemented Python program.

A. Advantages

The required type and scope of attacks can be defined individually as part of the attack planning process. This allows data sets to be created according to the user's needs. For example, very long attacks or many attacks, in short succession, can be carried out.

Unlike synthetically generated data, the actual sending of the packets ensures that the network data is correct and error-free. In addition, the network behavior during the attack is authentic. There are fewer potential sources of error in contrast to synthetically generated data, for example, by network simulators. Also in distinction from available DDoS data sets, the data can be generated variably and adjusted according to individual needs.

If a physic attack network were to be implemented for DDoS data generation, this would be accompanied by high material costs for the hardware. In contrast, the implemented Python program is a cost-efficient solution for data generation [15].

B. Limitations of DDoS Python implementation

The DDoS attack program is limited by the number of threads on the attack host. Real DDoS botnets include several thousand hosts. This is not feasible by multithreading with a single attack host. The data transfer rate with the Python program is also lower than in a DDoS attack with a resource-strong botnet.

C. Augmentation of the training data

For the purpose of training data generation, augmentation techniques are used to extend or adapt the existing training data set. The main weakness of the DDoS program is the limited simulatability of a large botnet. Therefore, it is a good idea to first generate a set of realistic DDoS attack datasets as large as possible and then use data manipulation to adjust the training data. Each packet in the network record has a timestamp at which it is captured.

By manipulating the timestamp, multiple attacks that occurred in succession can be combined into a parallel attack to represent a larger attack. This is only limited by the number of spoofed hosts. Augmentation can be done either as part of the package labelling process or retrospectively in the SQL database.

D. iIDS for defending against DDoS attacks

DDoS attacks are difficult to defend against, and existing defenses and prevention measures can be largely mitigated by the attacker. An iIDS is a promising approach.

It usually consists of various modules, which can detect network anomalies based on machine learning techniques and deviations from the usual network traffic of IoT devices. In addition to anomaly detection, the iIDS can classify attacks and distinguish between DDoS attacks and man-in-the-middle attacks [16]. In order to develop an own iIDS, extensive training data is needed. The implemented and described Python program is an approach to generate this training data.

VIII. Outlook

The Python program can be extended to include other DoS attack variants. Scapy allows the variable creation of any network packet. This allows ICMP flooding and HTTP flooding to be implemented. It is planned to split the attacks across multiple physical hosts to create a real distribution, in addition to the simulated distribution through multithreading. For this purpose, several Raspberry Pis are used to perform simultaneous attacks on a target. Subsequently, a larger field trial will be conducted to scale the data generation to a larger scale. Adding more attack hosts to the experimental setup gives a true distribution of the attack. In conjunction with multiple threads, this approaches a larger botnet.

To validate the generated data, it is planned to replicate publicly available DDoS datasets. Similar host quantity and variance will be used, also the packet quantity can be replicated. However, the packet transmission frequency is limited by the hardware on which the Python program runs. For further validation, we plan to create a test setup with an available IDS and train it with our data. This will allow us to compare the results of our system with the available one.

References

[1] Infosecurity Magazine, "DDoS Attacks in 2022: Trends and Obstacles Amid Worldwide Political Crisis," 2022. [Online]. Available: https://www.infosecurity-magazine.com/blogs/ddos-attacks-in-2022-trends/ (visited on 06/07/2023).

[2] C. Douligeris and A. Mitrokotsa, "DDoS attacks and defense mechanisms: Classification and state-of-the-art," en, *Computer Networks*, vol. 44, no. 5, pp. 643–666, Apr. 2004, ISSN: 13891286. DOI: 10.1016/j.comnet.2003.10.003. [Online]. Available: https://linkinghub.elsevier.com/retrieve/pii/S1389128603004250 (visited on 03/01/2023).

[3] N. Sidhu, K. Saluja, M. Sachdeva, and J. Singh, "Ddos attack's simulation using legitimate and attack real data sets," *J. Scientific And Engineering Research*, Jun. 2012.

[4] Research Scholar, SRM University, Sonepat, (Haryana) India., S. Arora*, D. S. Dalal, and Professor, Teerthanker Mahaveer University, Moradabad (U.P), India., "DDoS Attacks Simulation in Cloud Computing Environment," *International Journal of Innovative Technology and Exploring Engineering*, vol. 9, no. 1, pp. 414–417, Nov. 2019, ISSN: 22783075. DOI: 10.35940/ijitee.A4163.119119. [Online]. Available: https://www.ijitee.org/portfolio-item/A4163119119/ (visited on 05/10/2023).

[5] A. Balyk, M. Karpinski, A. Naglik, G. Shangytbayeva, and I. Romanets, "Using graphic network simulator 3 for ddos attacks simulation," *International Journal of Computing*, vol. 16, pp. 219–225, Dec. 2017. DOI: 10.47839/ijc.16.4.910.

[6] S. Alzahrani and L. Hong, "Generation of DDoS Attack Dataset for Effective IDS Development and Evaluation," *Journal of Information Security*, vol. 09, no. 04, pp. 225–241, 2018, ISSN: 2153-1234, 2153-1242. DOI: 10.4236/jis.2018.94016. [Online]. Available: http://www.scirp.org/journal/doi.aspx?DOI=10.4236/jis.2018.94016 (visited on 03/06/2023).

[7] *Global Journal of Computer Science and Technology*, vol. 14, no. E7, pp. 15–32, 2014, ISSN: 0975-4172. [Online]. Available: https://computerresearch.org/index.php/computer/article/view/100887.

[8] D. Mahajan and M. Sachdeva, "DDoS Attack Prevention and Mitigation Techniques - A Review," *International Journal of Computer Applications*, vol. 67, no. 19, pp. 21–24, 2013. DOI: 10.5120/11504-7221. [Online]. Available: https://www.researchgate.net/publication/258790077_DDoS_Attack_Prevention_and_Mitigation_Techniques_-_A_Review (visited on 06/07/2023).

[9] S. S. Kolahi, K. Treseangrat, and B. A. S. Sarrafpour, "Analysis of udp ddos flood cyber attack and defense mechanisms on web server with linux ubuntu 13," *2015 International Conference on Communications, Signal Processing, and their Applications (ICCSPA'15)*, pp. 1–5, 2015.

[10] A. N. S. Team, *2022 in review: DDoS attack trends and insights*, en-US, Feb. 2023. [Online]. Available: http://www.microsoft.com/en-us/security/blog/2023/02/21/2022-in-review-ddos-attack-trends-and-insights/ (visited on 03/01/2023).

[11] O. Yoachimik, "Cloudflare DDoS threat report for 2022 Q4," *The Cloudflare Blog*, 10.01.2023. [Online]. Available: https://blog.cloudflare.com/ddos-threat-report-2022-q4/ (visited on 06/07/2023).

[12] Kamaldeep, M. Malik, and M. Dutta, "Contiki-based mitigation of UDP flooding attacks in the Internet of things," in *2017 International Conference on Computing, Communication and Automation (ICCCA)*, Greater Noida: IEEE, May 2017, pp. 1296–1300, ISBN: 9781509064717. DOI: 10.1109/CCAA.2017.8229997. [Online]. Available: http://ieeexplore.ieee.org/document/8229997/ (visited on 03/01/2023).

[13] IETF Datatracker, *RFC ft-ietf-tcpm-rfc793bis: Transmission Control Protocol (TCP)*, 2022. [Online]. Available: https://datatracker.ietf.org/doc/html/rfc9293 (visited on 06/07/2023).

[14] *Defenses against TCP SYN flooding attacks.* 2006. [Online]. Available: https://www.netconf.co.uk/ipj/ipj_9-4.pdf (visited on 06/07/2023).

[15] S. Alzahrani and L. Hong, "Generation of ddos attack dataset for effective ids development and evaluation," *Journal of Information Security*, vol. 09, pp. 225–241, Jan. 2018. DOI: 10.4236/jis.2018.94016.

[16] J. Graf, K. Neubauer, S. Fischer, and R. Hackenberg, "Architecture of an intelligent intrusion detection system for smart home," in *2020 IEEE International Conference on Pervasive Computing and Communications Workshops (PerCom Workshops)*, 2020, pp. 1–6. DOI: 10.1109/PerComWorkshops48775.2020.9156168.

Side Channel Monitoring for Fuzz Testing of Future Mobility Systems

Philipp Fuxen
Dept. Informatics and Mathematics
OTH Regensburg
Regensburg, Germany
Email: Philipp.Fuxen@oth-regensburg.de

Murad Hachani
Dept. Informatics and Mathematics
OTH Regensburg
Regensburg, Germany
Email: Murad.Hachani@oth-regensburg.de

Jonas Schmidt
Dept. Informatics and Mathematics
OTH Regensburg
Regensburg, Germany
Email: Jonas.Schmidt.lth@t-online.de

Philipp Zaumseil
Dept. Informatics and Mathematics
OTH Regensburg
Regensburg, Germany
Email: Philipp.Zaumseil@st.oth-regensburg.de

Rudolf Hackenberg
Dept. Informatics and Mathematics
OTH Regensburg
Regensburg, Germany
Email: Rudolf.Hackenberg@oth-regensburg.de

***Abstract*—The current transformation in the automotive industry is leading to new technologies with a higher software content, a higher degree of networking, and connections to cloud services. This development leads to an increase in the attack surface and the potential extent of damage. ISO/SAE 21434 and UNECE WP.29/R155 were published to address this development. The ISO/SAE 21434 proposes fuzz testing as a measure. In fuzzing, so-called fuzz data is generated and transmitted to a device under test to identify previously unknown and known vulnerabilities. This approach is already being used very successfully in other industries. But in the automotive sector, some challenges arise when testing hardware-related electronic control units. These include the fact that the internal system structures are often poorly known or not known, as well as the severely restricted access and hardware limitations for monitoring. One way to solve these challenges is to use side-channel information to monitor the device under test. Such information includes power consumption, temperature, and noise levels, for example. In this paper, we present a fuzz testing experiment to determine anomalies, data, and requirements for analyzing various side channels. Basic procedures were used to generate the fuzz data. Monitoring of the device under test was performed manually at the beginning. In addition, a side-channel measurement system with various measurement devices and a test setup are presented. Based on the identified fuzz messages, the behavior of the respective side channels during the abnormal behavior is analyzed and described.**

Keywords*—*Fuzzing; Fuzz Testing; Automotive; Cybersecurity; Side Channel Information; Measurement System.

I. Introduction

The four major themes of future mobility - Connected, Autonomous, Shared, and Electric - have brought a transformation in the automotive industry [1]. New technologies with high software content and a high degree of networking have become established. In addition to the added value, however, this also leads to new risks. The vehicle has evolved into a highly networked system which is connected with multiple cloud services, and whose attack surface has grown significantly. This has increased the probability of becoming the target of an attack on cybersecurity. In the past, attackers had to gain physical access to a vehicle to manipulate it. Today, remote access to a vehicle can be carried out through a communication channel or a cloud backend. In addition to increasing the probability of occurrence, this also means that the extent of damage is significantly greater because attacks could be extended to fleets of vehicles.

In recent years, the international standard ISO/SAE 21434 and the european standard UNECE WP.29/R155 have been developed to address this issue [2][3]. The ISO/SAE 21434 defines a framework of technical requirements for cybersecurity and risk management to ensure the cybersecurity of motor vehicles throughout their life cycle. It covers concepts, product development, production, operation, maintenance, and decommissioning of Electric / Electronic (E/E) vehicle systems. A test method proposed by ISO/SAE 21434 that is suitable for automated execution is the so-called fuzz testing. It is already used successfully in other industries and makes it possible to identify even previously unknown weaknesses and vulnerabilities [4]. A fuzz tester generates so-called fuzz data and transmits it to the System Under Test (SUT) or Device Under Test (DUT). Some fuzzers look for faults and anomalies while the SUT/DUT processes the fuzz data. The goal is to find out what fuzz data causes unwanted system behavior. The data is then analyzed to see if there is a vulnerability. To use fuzz tests automatically and efficiently for automotive systems, it is necessary to detect abnormal behavior of the DUT. This is particularly difficult for automotive Electronic Control Unit (ECU) because there is often little or no knowledge of the internal processes during testing. In addition, their monitoring is a challenge due to highly restricted access and hardware limitations. So-called black box methods are therefore particularly relevant in the automotive sector. Compared to white box or grey box methods, no initial information about the DUT is required.

The main goal of the paper is to improve black box protocol

fuzz testing for hardware-based automotive systems using side channel information. For this reason, the following research questions are addressed:

RQ1: How can fuzz messages be found which have led to abnormal behavior?

RQ2: Which side channels are suitable to use for automotive ECUs?

RQ3: How can this side channel information be measured and used?

The structure of the paper begins with related work in Section II. Section III presents the general conditions of an experiment and its setup as well as its results. In Section IV, a side channel measurement system is described that is designed to solve the challenges of hardware-based fuzzing. The paper ends with a conclusion and future work in Section V and Section VI.

II. Related Work

During fuzz testing of complex and networked vehicle systems, obtaining information about the state of the ECU is difficult. The main reason for this is that access to the ECU is limited and very few information channels are open or available. One method for monitoring during fuzz testing is the so-called side channel information, which has already been successfully used in other areas.

A. *Side Channel Analysis*

Side channel analysis is a technique for detecting vulnerabilities in a system by analyzing information that can be measured through side channels. D. Agrawal et al. [5] present multichannel attacks, i.e., attacks that use multiple side channels. These attack types use more than one side channel, e.g., energy and Electromagnetic Fields (EMF), in parallel. Based on their analysis, they show that using multiple channels is better for template attacks by experimentally demonstrating a threefold reduction in error probability. In this work, the transfer to ECUs was performed by connecting a large number of side channels. In particular, the analysis of the temperature and electromagnetic radiation of the power showed clear results for reverse engineering cryptographic functions [6][7]. Therefore, the application of these side channels found use in our setup right at the beginning.

B. *General Fuzzing*

As stated in Section I, fuzzers can be classified into three test procedures based on their knowledge about the system: black box, grey box, and white box fuzzing [8][9]. The following papers present various fuzzing approches from the diffrent test procedures.

M. Böhme et al. [10] present a comprehensive synthesis of the open challenges and opportunities associated with fuzzing and symbolic execution techniques. These problems were identified through a discourse between researchers and practitioners during a Shonan meeting and confirmed by a follow-up survey. They used the term human-in-the-loop for an issue, defined as the work effort that an test auditor has to perform within a semi-automatic fuzzing loop. This was also confirmed by their survey, where 71% of the participants indicated that there is potential to improve the automation of such fuzzing mechanisms. As we move forward, we focus on addressing this issue by automating most of the evaluation steps with Artificial Intelligence (AI) in our future work.

L. McDonald et al. [9] synthesize the current state of the art in fuzzing approaches, classify these approaches, and highlight key insights into the current state of research as well as current challenges. After comparing the current state of the art in fuzzing methods, including hybrid fuzzing, which combines a static analysis of the program and the discovering of bugs during runtime, symbolic execution, which discovers new execution paths by tracking symbolic inputs and machine learning approaches. They continued their future work by highlighting the threats associated with the transition to cyber-physical systems, such as fully automated cars and smart power grids. They presented several options that extend fuzzing as a useful test technique. In the context of embedded systems, they explained that fuzzing using side channels is a suitable mechanism to make black box testing more efficient. In Section II-C we will focus on these approaches and afterward try to research adaptions to the automotive sector in Section II-D.

C. *Side Channel Fuzzing*

The increasing popularity of efficient fuzzing methods in the embedded systems domain is leading to the identification of new barriers to test automation. These often include a lack of Input / Output (I/O) capabilities, limited computational capacity, and the lack of an operating system in most cases [11][12]. In combination, this results mainly in a black box view of the system. However, in order to implement the three-stage process of fuzzing and thus guarantee a higher level of fault detection, feedback information in the form of side channels has to be applied. These can subsequently be supplied to the fuzzer as input in order to be able to continuously adapt to subsequent test cycles. P. Sperl et al. [11] present a new approach to extract feedback for fuzzing on embedded devices using the information on the power consumption leaks. They carried out their proof of concept by fuzzing synthetic software and a lightweight Advanced Encryption Standard (AES) implementation running on an ARM Cortex-M4 microcontroller. Focusing on detecting various vulnerabilities in an ECU and combining different side channels, less cryptographic analysis of side channel information was completed and more emphasis was on detecting unexpected anomalous behavior.

D. *Fuzzing of Automotive ECUs*

The implementation of fuzzing within the Controller Area Network (CAN) protocol is an area that has already been widely represented. The publication by P. Patki et al. [13] discusses the importance of penetration testing (pen testing) in finding vulnerabilities in enterprise and automotive networks. The proposed fuzzing tool uses a mutation-based approach for invalid input creation for CAN. The mutation-based approaches use seeds, which are initial inputs, and then modify them according to a mutation algorithm. According to H. Lee et al. [14], no form of prior knowledge was necessary for fuzzing the CAN protocol. They describe a two-step process that involved, on the one hand, scanning and analyzing the CAN traffic on the CAN bus and, on the other hand, forming completely randomized messages. The packets were injected into the CAN bus via a Bluetooth interface. They were able to attack sophisticated ECUs and change the behaviors of the vehicle. Without intelligent mechanisms for automated evaluation, these procedures require a high degree of manual observation and analysis. We are trying to improve process capability by introducing a fully automated cycle for test automation. M. Dunne et al. [15] introduced a so-called hardware-in-the-loop system for fuzzing a CAN-connected system. For this purpose, monitoring of the power trace was implemented as a side channel. They demonstrate that this black box approach can be used to detect responses to messages.

In summary, through our extension of the side channels, which are specified in Section IV, and the resulting enrichment of the system's feedback information, we aim to increase the coverage of detectable error sources and vulnerabilities. Through the automated cycle, we take the approach of reducing manual analysis to increase data throughput and speed.

III. Experiment

In this Section, we describe the implementation of the fuzzing experiment and its results. It was conducted to collect anomalies and data for later evaluation of the side channels. Furthermore, requirements for the implementation of a fuzzer are collected during the execution. The fuzzing of the CAN channels of an automotive ECU is started. In this process, the ECU was observed manually and with basic analysis methods. An anomaly was detected when the ECU behaved in a way that deviated from the normal operating state.

A. Hardware Setup

In order for the experiment to be carried out, the hardware must first be connected to the automotive ECU. Therefore, it must be supplied with voltage on the one hand and the CAN bus must be connected to a computer on the other. For the connection between the computer and the CAN bus of the ECU, a so-called CAN-to-Universal Serial Bus (USB) interface was used. Specifically, the OWASP Automotive EMB 60 was used, which is available as an open-source project [16]. Therefore, hardware and software can be accessed. It provides two Controller Area Network Flexible Data Rate (CAN FD) channels connected via a single D-sub 9 connector. Connection to the computer is via a USB 1.0/2.0 type B connector.

As shown in Figure 1, in addition to the computer and the CAN interface, a laboratory power supply is also needed to ensure the supply voltage of the control unit. To connect these, the corresponding connection pins on the control unit for Voltage Common Collector (VCC) and Ground (GND) were measured with a multimeter. These were then wired to the laboratory power supply with VCC and GND. A residual

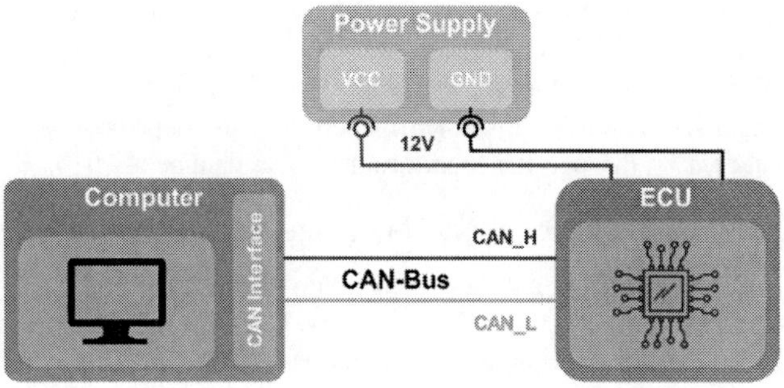

Figure 1. Hardware Setup.

bus simulation or similar is not required for the control unit, as it is integrated into a dedicated experimental setup.

B. Fuzzing Test

For carrying out the fuzzing test, some software is also required on the computer. A Linux distribution serves as the operating system. To use the CAN-to-USB interface, the kernel interface SocketCAN is utilized. To be able to run SocketCAN via the Linux console for the CAN functionality, the package can-utils is installed. The Python programming language is suitable for programming fuzzing scripts. The Python package python-can enables the CAN functionality.

At the beginning of the experiment, so-called random fuzzing was implemented with the Python library python-can. Randomly generated CAN frames were sent to the ECU. In addition to the basic random fuzz tests, protocol-specific areas were analyzed and tested with random values according to the limits. The random analysis of individual features and communication paths of the CAN protocol already provided initial results. The monitoring of the system behavior was carried out manually during the experiment. For this purpose, the dedicated experimental setup of the ECU was observed, equipped with several infotainment displays and an instrument cluster. These indicate changes when the fuzzy CAN frames are sent. Moreover, the breakdown of the displays indicates a potential crash of the system.

In addition to the self-implemented random fuzzing, tests were also carried out with Scapy. Scapy is a python library, which is utilized for the manipulation and analysis of network packages. Caring Caribou, which is an open source fuzzer, was also used to identify anomalies. Its fuzzer module has three modes for generating fuzz data: Random, brute, and mutate. Besides generating fuzz data, Caring Caribou also has a function to identify messages that have triggered anomalous behavior. For identification, the transmitted fuzz messages are played back block by block. The user can indicate whether the observed behavior occurred in a block. If this is the case, the block is divided into smaller blocks and replayed. This process continues until the message is identified [17][18].

The fuzz messages identified and classified as anomalies form the basis for further work. With the help of the detected abnormal behaviors, the side channel information can be analyzed and training data for AI models can be generated. Identifying the relationship between a fuzz message and the associated abnormal behavior proved to be very tedious without a monitoring system. Therefore, an improvement is necessary through the monitoring of side channels.

IV. Side Channel Measurement System

The optimization of new application-oriented fuzzing mechanisms for automotive ECUs, as well as the consideration of these hardware-related systems as a black box, requires the extraction of information through the connection of side channels. Previous methods and applications of fuzzing often involved the self-performed observation and evaluation of system responses to classify a vulnerability based on the results. To ensure a standardized and secure development process according to ISO/SAE 21434, an automated approach is essential. Only an automated evaluation and adaptation of the fuzzing and its results enables a high coverage of the detectable vulnerabilities. Based on the assumption that the efficiency and correctness of our fuzzing unit increase proportionally with the amount of information that can be extracted from the system in the form of side channels, we used further side channels for the analysis of the DUT in addition to the established analysis of the power traces.

Figure 2. Side Channel Measurement.

Figure 2 shows our setup with the measuring devices included. The ECU is visible in the center, which is connected to the rest infotainment system and to the side channel measuring devices. These are described in the following sections. In addition to the measurement setup, the Grafana dashboard can also be seen, as it is described in more detail in Section IV-G.

A. Power

The analysis of power traces as a side channel achieved remarkable results, especially in the field of cryptography. For reverse engineering applications, the analysis of this side channel proved to be a useful instrument to draw conclusions about program structures and functional flows. In the context of fuzzing and the consideration of the DUT as a black box, the detection of anomalies in the power trace and the interpretation of the fuzzer's input serve to uncover vulnerabilities.

The acquisition of the power trace is done by connecting an oscilloscope. The current intensity is measured, which the control unit requires during the input phase of data generated by the fuzzer. With randomized fuzzing, it was already possible to identify a bug by the history of the measurement of the power consumption and the voltage. The visualization in Grafana shows a drop in voltage, which was related to the simultaneous crash of the infotainment displays. After a few seconds, an automatic reset of the ECU could be detected in the measurement. After the restart, the voltage, as well as the power consumption, fluctuated from the normal state.

B. CAN

In addition to the physical data, software, and protocol-specific data can also be recorded. This data is not measured via a sensor but is directly acquired by the system or the communication protocol. In the case of the CAN protocol, several side channel features can be calculated. These include bus load, message frequency per ID, or bit flip rate. These metrics are added to the data stream as measured values.

When monitoring the DUT during fuzz testing, the side channel features of the CAN are used to detect changes in communication behavior. For example, when analyzing an anomaly, the bus load was found to dip and then return to normal shortly thereafter.

C. Thermal Image

The use of infrared images is increasingly applied in a wide range of applications. Due to the rich information content paired with the wide range of areas of application, the use of infrared images proved to be a good tool for the detection of anomalies. Usually, reference values in the form of patterns within images or plain temperature values are used to successfully detect an anomaly. For the adaptation to embedded systems and especially ECUs in the automotive domain, preparations have to take place in the way of exposing components of interest. By exposing components and so-called regions of interest, the focus of anomaly detection can be explicitly set on CAN-related components, for example.

Using direct fuzzing on specific areas of the CAN protocol, significant differences in the heat signatures could already be detected manually. Unusual temperature patterns were measured in the area of the CAN controller and the Central Processing Unit (CPU). The temperature increased significantly compared to the normal state.

D. Temperature

The need to expose components leads to a reduction of the potentially measurable area. In order to compensate for this limitation of the thermal camera, temperature sensors offer a remedy. By subdividing the DUT into measuring ranges and placing individual sensors in a controlled manner, maximum measurement coverage of relevant areas can be achieved. Combined with visual patterns, a larger data space for the temperature side channel is created, facilitating the contribution and application of AI techniques.

Like the detection by infrared images described previously, the same effect could be measured by the stationarily installed temperature sensors. A clear increase could be analyzed, which also deviates considerably from the normal state.

E. Visual Image

The input to an ECU by fuzzer-generated messages produces different reactions depending on the communication protocol and the task of the ECU. Manual examination of the ECU's response and reaction to fuzzer-generated messages allows an anomaly to be accurately detected, yet the effort involved is too high. Visual and automated examination by connecting a camera that monitors the system can substitute this process. The functionality for anomaly detection is limited to the detection of movements, changes in structure, and other visual features. Relevant values for recording are the image sequence, which was identified as an anomaly, and a value that indicates an anomaly.

As described in Section IV-A, it was possible to see a parallel to the crash of the displays and an anomaly within the measurements. This connection could be created by performing an observation of the outputs on the displays of the test bench. Through automated observation and anomaly detection, the following anomalies, brought about by random fuzzing, could be detected. Firstly, flickering and abnormal changes in driving modes could be detected. Secondly, repeated crashes could be detected by the camera.

F. Acoustic

Besides the already mentioned side channels, there are also indicators that can be recorded via the acoustic channel. The rotation of the ECU fan can indicate the processor load. After all, as computing power increases, so does the temperature of the CPU, which is cooled by the controller's fan. Consequently, an unexpectedly high fan speed is synonymous with a code execution anomaly. Since the fan produces a certain noise depending on the workload, measuring this noise is a way to draw conclusions about the fan's speed. Noise and other irritations can be avoided by placing a microphone next to the fan. The rotation and resulting noise of the fan thus represent the dominant frequency in the measurement. This can then be isolated and analyzed without adding other noise. Performing fuzzing randomly also led to the detection of an anomaly in the fan's measurement. When the anomaly occurred, the fuzzer gradually increased the speed of the fan. The increase in speed from normal was not stopped when the anomaly occurred. Accordingly, the fan remained in this mode even after several hours without resetting.

G. Visualization

The connection of a wide variety of side channels led to increased complexity in the evaluation of the combined side channels. The uniform and central data collection as a data lake is the basic building block for subsequent analyses. The data lake was implemented in the form of an Influx database, which enables the transfer of measured values in near real time. Based on the visualization of the data with Grafana, as shown in Figure 3, first explorative analyses can be performed on the measurement data. In this way, initial findings could be obtained. In addition, the centralized data storage achieves preparation for further analysis methods for anomaly detection (Machine learning and deep learning).

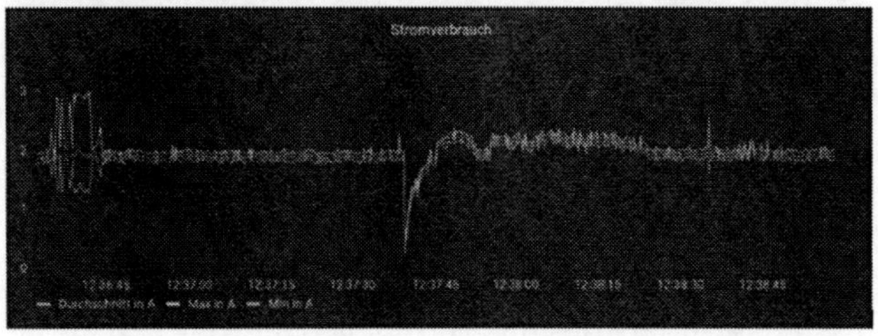

Figure 3. Power Consumption Widget of Grafana Dashboard.

Figure 3 represents exemplary the visual processing of the measured power consumption as a time series. A visually identifiable anomaly can be seen within the depicted time frame. The fuzzing of the ECU started at time 12:36:30 and caused a shutdown, which triggered at time 12:37:40. After rebooting the ECU, a normal condition could not be established. This anomaly can already be detected by applying simple algorithms within the measurement system and offers the possibility to generate a dedicated feedback for the fuzzer. In addition to the various physical side channel data, CAN messages are also recorded to find correlations between anomalies and received messages.

V. CONCLUSION

The current turnaround in the automotive sector is leading to the introduction of new technologies with significantly more software and connectivity. This increases the attack surface and the damage potential. One standard that counteracts this development is ISO/SAE 21434, which regulates the cybersecurity of vehicles over their entire life cycle. One of the measures it proposes is fuzz testing. In other industries, fuzz tests are already being used very successfully. However, in the automotive sector, some challenges arise due to hardware-related ECUs.

The approach taken in this paper aims to solve these problems using side channel information processing. These are already being used successfully in several areas. Therefore, the Section on related work has been divided into the following structure: side channel analysis, general fuzzing, side channel fuzzing, and fuzzing of automotive ECUs. In the subsections, various relevant approaches have been discussed, which are in the context of this paper.

To collect anomalies, data, and requirements for evaluating the different side channels, a fuzzing experiment was conducted.CAN was used as the communication protocol to be fuzzed. Fuzz data generation was performed using a self-programmed random fuzzer and the two frameworks Caring Caribou and Scapy. The monitoring of system behavior was performed manually for the time being. Detect the relationship between a fuzz message and an anomaly is tedious. The discovered fuzz messages and the corresponding anomalies are used for the later analysis of the side channels and for the dataset creation.

A measurement system with several sensors and interfaces was built to measure side channel data. This was connected to a test setup. Methods, such as the analysis of power and temperature were used. To achieve a high degree of coverage of temperature information, temperature sensors were used in addition to a thermal imaging camera. These were placed in areas that could not be detected by the thermal imaging camera. In addition, a microphone was installed in such a way that the frequency of the control unit fan was recorded. A camera was used to record the multimedia displays and the instrument cluster of the test bench. With a CAN interface, various bus-specific side channel information could be obtained. By combining the different side channels, the information content is increased because not every abnormality is noticed on every side channel. The detection of anomalies during monitoring thus has a broad database.

VI. Future Work

Since the current measurement system implements only part of the fuzzing cycle, further process steps must be performed to complete the fuzzer. Based on the data from the measurement system, static analyses are first performed. After these analyses, more intelligent methods (Machine learning and deep learning) for monitoring the fuzzed DUT will be investigated and implemented.

In the next phase, fuzz data generation will be extended from random generation and block-based generation to feedback-based generation. To this end, the fuzz data generation will be adjusted according to the feedback from the monitoring system to find anomalies more efficiently. This is to achieve deeper program structures and the system architecture.

References

[1] U. Z. Abdul Hamid, *Autonomous, Connected, Electric and Shared Vehicles: Disrupting the Automotive and Mobility Sectors*. Warrendale, Pennsylvania, USA: SAE International, Oct. 2022, ISBN: 978-1-4686-0347-7.

[2] "ISO/SAE 21434:2021 Road vehicles — Cybersecurity engineering," International Organization for Standardization and SAE International, Standard, Aug. 2021.

[3] "UN Regulation No. 155 - Cyber security and cyber security management system," United Nations Economic Commission for Europe, Standard, Mar. 2021.

[4] N. Besic, *Fuzzing: The Next Big Thing in Cybersecurity? - Bright Security*, May 2022. [Online]. Available: https://brightsec.com/blog/fuzzing/ (retrieved: 2023-06-08).

[5] D. Agrawal, J. R. Rao, and P. Rohatgi, "Multi-channel attacks," in *Cryptographic Hardware and Embedded Systems - CHES 2003*, ser. Lecture Notes in Computer Science, vol. 2779, Springer, Sep. 2003, pp. 2–16. DOI: 10.1007/978-3-540-45238-6_2.

[6] M. Hutter and J.-M. Schmidt, "The temperature side channel and heating fault attacks," in *Smart Card Research and Advanced Applications - CARDIS 2013*, Nov. 2014, pp. 219–235, ISBN: 978-3-319-08301-8. DOI: 10.1007/978-3-319-08302-5_15.

[7] K. Gandolfi, C. Mourtel, and F. Olivier, "Electromagnetic analysis: Concrete results," in *Cryptographic Hardware and Embedded Systems - CHES 2001*, ser. Lecture Notes in Computer Science, vol. 2162, Springer, May 2001, pp. 251–261. DOI: 10.1007/3-540-44709-1_21.

[8] J. Li, B. Zhao, and C. Zhang, "Fuzzing: A survey," *Cybersecurity*, vol. 1, no. 6, Jun. 2018. DOI: 10.1186/s42400-018-0002-y.

[9] A. Barkworth, L. Mcdonald, and M. Ijaz Ul Haq, "Survey of software fuzzing techniques," Dec. 2021.

[10] M. Böhme, C. Cadar, and A. Roychoudhury, "Fuzzing: Challenges and reflections," *IEEE Software*, vol. 38, no. 3, pp. 79–86, 2021.

[11] P. Sperl and K. Böttinger, "Side-channel aware fuzzing," in *Computer Security–ESORICS 2019: European Symposium on Research in Computer Security*, Springer, vol. 24, Sep. 2019, pp. 259–278, ISBN: 978-3-030-29958-3. DOI: 10.1007/978-3-030-29959-0_13.

[12] M. Muench, J. Stijohann, F. Kargl, A. Francillon, and D. Balzarotti, "What you corrupt is not what you crash: Challenges in fuzzing embedded devices," Jan. 2018. DOI: 10.14722/ndss.2018.23176.

[13] P. Patki, A. Gotkhindikar, and S. Mane, "Intelligent fuzz testing framework for finding hidden vulnerabilities in automotive environment," in *2018 Fourth International Conference on Computing Communication Control and Automation (ICCUBEA)*, vol. 4, IEEE, 2018, pp. 1–4.

[14] H. Lee, K. Choi, K. Chung, J. Kim, and K. Yim, "Fuzzing can packets into automobiles," in *IEEE International Conference on Advanced Information Networking and Applications*, vol. 29, IEEE, 2015, pp. 817–821.

[15] M. Dunne and S. Fischmeister, "Powertrace-based fuzzing of can connected hardware," in *2022 IEEE International Conference on Cyber Security and Resilience (CSR)*, IEEE, 2022, pp. 239–244.

[16] A. Meisel, *Owasp automotive emb 60 — owasp foundation*. [Online]. Available: https://owasp.org/www-project-automotive-emb-60/ (retrieved: 2023-06-08).

[17] mjidhage, kasperkarlsson, TobLans, *et al.*, *Documentation for caring caribou*. [Online]. Available: https://github.com/CaringCaribou/caringcaribou/blob/master/README.md (retrieved: 2023-06-08).

[18] P. Biondi, *Scapy: The python-based interactive packet manipulation program & library*. [Online]. Available: https://scapy.readthedocs.io/en/latest/index.html (retrieved: 2023-06-08).

Security Challenges for Cloud or Fog computing-Based AI Applications

Amir Pakmehr*, Andreas Aßmuth†, Christoph P. Neumann†, and Gerald Pirkl†

*Department of Computer and Information Technology Engineering
Qazvin Branch, Islamic Azad University, Qazvin, Iran
E-mail: amir.pakmehr@QIAU.ac.ir
†Department of Electrical Engineering, Media and Computer Science
Ostbayerische Technische Hochschule Amberg-Weiden, Amberg, Germany
E-mail: {a.assmuth | c.neumann | g.pirkl}@oth-aw.de

***Abstract*—Security challenges for cloud or fog-based machine learning services pose several concerns. Securing the underlying cloud or fog services is essential, as successful attacks against these services, on which machine learning applications rely, can lead to significant impairments of these applications. Because the requirements for Artificial Intelligence applications can also be different, we differentiate according to whether they are used in the cloud or in a fog computing network. This then also results in different threats or attack possibilities. For cloud platforms, the responsibility for security can be divided between different parties. Security deficiencies at a lower level can have a direct impact on the higher level where user data is stored. While responsibilities are simpler for fog computing networks, by moving services to the edge of the network, we have to secure them against physical access to the devices. We conclude by outlining specific information security requirements for Artificial Intelligence applications.**

Keywords-cybersecurity; cloud; fog; machine learning applications.

I. Introduction

At the latest, since the presentation of ChatGPT by OpenAI in November 2022, the topic of Artificial Intelligence (AI) has been present and interesting even among a non-specialist audience. It is somewhat misunderstood that Machine Learning (ML) has already been used for more and more services in the private, commercial and industrial sectors in recent years – and the trend is rising. For many ML applications, cloud services are quite central as they provide a fast, scalable, flexible and cost-effective infrastructure for running sophisticated ML models and algorithms. Through them, enterprises can successfully and efficiently implement their ML projects. Some of the key benefits of cloud services for ML are:

1) **Scalability**: Cloud services make it possible to scale up the required computing power to meet the requirements of the respective ML application. This is not only about the execution of the ML application, also the training of the models can be pushed by additional computing power or more available memory for larger amounts of data. Elasticity allows to scale down the computing resources, when they are not needed any more.
2) **Flexibility**: There is a great versatility in the ML services offered, like cloud-based machine learning development platforms in general, but also dedicated ML services for text-to-speech, speech-to-text, translation, conversations, automated image and video analysis, and many more. Cloud offerings include infrastructure, platform, and software, which can be customized to suit the needs of different users and applications. Different deployment options for ML applications exist, such as container orchestration, virtual machines, or serverless computing.
3) **Cost efficiency**: Companies that deploy ML applications do not have to buy required hardware and perpetual licenses themselves or pay for its operation, but they can rent computing power or storage as well as subscription-based licenses. The Cloud Service Providers (CSP) offer more fine-grained cost models than traditional data centers. In combination with elasticity, they allow for pay-as-you-go or pay-as-you-grow approaches, which can result in lower costs. The CSPs offer their ML services worldwide, thus, international distribution of enterprise ML products becomes cost efficient.
4) **Data management**: Cloud services can store and process large amounts of data that usually accompany modern ML applications.
5) **Integration**: Cloud services, as a now established technology, offer a variety of other established tools and services, e.g., visualization tools, connection to databases, or workflow engines, making it easy to seamlessly integrate ML applications into existing web-based services or even an IT infrastructure.

However, a generalization that AI and ML applications are only possible with cloud services is not permissible. There are also other areas of application for ML, like autonomous driving, in which a connection to cloud services is not continuously possible or does not make sense in large parts. In autonomous driving, the merging of image and radar data on the current traffic situation of a vehicle must take place in real time. Particularly when human life and limb are at stake, for example, when emergency braking is required, there is no time to first transfer all image and radar data to the cloud, analyzing it using ML algorithms, come up with the "brake at once" decision, and transmit the command to trigger the braking process to the vehicle. Thus, it is imperative to already have sufficient computing power and memory in the vehicle that all processing, computation and decision-making can take place on the spot. In so-called edge computing, the processing of data and the execution of applications is generally done on edge devices or devices close to the data sources, instead of being processed somewhere in the cloud. As the above example should make clear, criteria, such as real-time capability or minimal latency, are often crucial for such applications. Still, cloud services are part of the autonomous driving ecosystem, e.g., the higher-level control of traffic flow in a particular region, which uses swarm data retrieved from connected cars or the provision of map and navigation services in the vehicles.

An argument against cloud services and in favor of on-premise hardware commonly is better control over data protection and information security. However, even domains with strict regulations on security, like healthcare and banking, have adopted cloud services for some applications [1]. If regulations or trusted hardware considerations require in-depth control, private clouds involve setting up a cloud infrastructure that is dedicated to one's organization and is not shared with others.

Other reasons for having the processing of data and the execution of applications closer to the source of the data rather than in the cloud brings us to fog computing that aims to extend cloud computing capabilities to Internet of Things (IoT) devices and other edge devices, such as routers, switches, and gateways. It aims to provide a "foggy" layer of computing resources between the cloud and the edge, much like fog lies between the ground and the sky. The fog layer can help to reduce the latency and bandwidth requirements of cloud computing [2].

An example of an ML application deployed in the context of fog computing can be the processing of sensor data in a smart grid system. A smart grid is an electrical network that uses sensors and smart devices to monitor and optimize energy consumption. These sensors collect data, such as power consumption, network load, electricity price, power generation from renewable sources, and weather forecasts. In a typical fog computing architecture, the sensor data can be processed and analyzed at the edge devices in the smart grid. ML models trained on the sensor data can make predictions about energy demand and perform appropriate optimizations. By processing the data at the edge, real-time optimization of the power grid can be achieved without having to send all (possibly privacy-critical) data to a remote cloud. This can reduce latency and improve system efficiency. In addition, the fog computing network helps increase the security of the smart grid by eliminating the need to transmit data over public networks. Sensitive data remains on the edge device and can be better protected from potential attacks.

An essential prerequisite for the correct functioning of ML applications is correctly working and reliable cloud services or fog computing networks. Conversely, it is clear that the compromise of cloud services or a fog computing network will lead to massive problems for ML applications. Therefore, in this paper, we would like to present the security challenges for ML applications that are based on cloud or fog computing and provide guidance and best practice recommendations on how to mitigate or control the respective threats.

The paper is structured in the following manner: Section II discusses security challenges in cloud computing. Section III presents security challenges in fog computing. Finally, Section IV addresses special security challenges for ML applications in cloud or fog environments. The paper ends with a conclusion and an outlook on future work.

II. Cloud Computing Security Challenges

With regard to the correct functioning of ML services provided over the Internet, securing the underlying cloud services plays a very important role. Successful attacks against the cloud services on which ML applications rely can lead to significant impairments of these applications. But this is not the only reason why cloud services must be sensibly secured against cyberattacks. In practice, the fact that several parties are usually involved in the provision of cloud services often proves to be problematic. The classic Cloud Security Responsibility Model (CSRM) basically differentiates responsibility according to cloud vendor and user, distinguished for the service models Infrastructure as a Service (IaaS), Platform as a Service (PaaS) and Software as a Service (SaaS) [3]. Regardless of how many parties share responsibility for the cybersecurity of a cloud service, it is fundamental to ensure that responsibility at the interfaces between different parties in particular is clearly defined, because a security problem in one party's responsibility could potentially threaten the security of other parties' areas of responsibility. Due to the layer model of the system architecture, it is obvious that security deficiencies at a lower level have a direct impact on the higher level where, for example, user data is stored.

At the Cloud Computing 2019 conference, Süß et al. presented an overview of information security challenges for cloud services at the time and assessed them using the Common Vulnerability Scoring System (CVSS) [4]. However, when the Covid-19 pandemic began in early 2020, the security threats to cloud services changed. As many companies and organizations became more reliant on cloud services in a relatively short period of time because everyone's life was moved to the cloud, cybercriminals took advantage of this and tried to exploit vulnerabilities in cloud infrastructures. Very often, these were classic attacks that can also be used to attack other web services.

A. Data Breaches

First, we look at attacks that specifically target data stored in the cloud. This could be customer data, secret company documents or medical records on patients. In a data breach, unauthorized access to sensitive data is given, which, of course, can have serious consequences for businesses and individuals [5]. Data breaches can be the result of unintentional exposure of sensitive data due to misconfigurations or weak security measures [6] or a targeted attack. Data breaches usually result in the confidence of customers and business partners in the affected company being shaken, often coupled with a serious loss of reputation among the general public. Since the occurrence of a data leak usually involves a violation of compliance requirements and laws, such as the EU General Data Protection Regulation (GDPR), the affected companies usually have to fear regulatory consequences. In addition to fines, there may also be indemnity claims with a simultaneous loss of revenue. A data breach often leads to further impairment of business activities. For example, it would be similarly bad if such corporate data were accidentally deleted by an inattentive employee or deliberately by an attacker.

It should be noted that many cloud services that were used during the pandemic are still being used – which certainly makes sense. Although it is clear that by encrypting data that is stored in the cloud and implementation of a strict access control, one can guard against data breaches, their number and extent over the past two years (see [7] or [8], for example) is frightening, even though the first year of the Covid-19 pandemic has been called the "worst year on record" in terms of data leaks [9].

B. Ransomware Attacks

A so-called ransomware attack is an attack in which the attacker uses special malware to encrypt the victim's data and extort it by demanding payment for the surrender of the key. Probably the best known example of a ransomware attack was the WannaCry attack in 2017 which targeted computers running Microsoft Windows, encrypted the users data and demanded ransom payments in Bitcoin [10]. While early ransomware variants often encrypted only a user's data stored on the local hard drive, variants soon developed that also encrypted connected disks or cloud-based storage [11].

In addition to this general description of ransomware, it should be noted that the "Ransomware as a Service (RaaS)" business model has gained significant importance in recent years. Here, ransomware developers sell their malware as a service to criminals. RaaS platforms often offer various options that allow criminals to create and execute their own ransomware campaigns [12]. Such platforms often allow the customization of the ransomware, like the selection of targets or the determination of the ransom amount. Such services target less tech-savvy criminals, thereby enabling a wider range of people to run such ransomware campaigns. This increases the risk of ransomware attacks for all types of IT systems and, thus, also cloud services. We have already pointed out that in the case of cyberattacks on cloud services, responsibilities may be divided among several parties. Ransomware attacks are no exception in this regard. A user's data stored in the cloud could be encrypted as a result of catching a malicious ransomware on their PC or mobile device. In such a case, the responsibility is relatively clear and the CSP usually cannot help in such cases, unless the cloud storage service includes regular backups, and it is possible to restore a previous state of the data after removing the ransomware from the user's devices. In the event of an attack on the CSP during which the data of several (probably many) customers is encrypted, the responsibility lies with the CSP.

The best protection against ransomware attacks is to keep all software up to date in combination with regular backups. It is mandatory to install security updates as soon as they become available, because adversaries often exploit vulnerabilities in outdated software. This also comprises anti-virus software being constantly updated. Backups are mandatory, because even if a user sees no other way out than to pay the demanded ransom, this is no guarantee to get their own data back intact, of course. How much do you trust the promise of a criminal who has blackmailed you?

C. Distributed Denial of Service

In a Distributed Denial of Service (DDoS) attack, a target system is flooded by mass requests. The bandwidth of the service's connection to the Internet is no longer sufficient, so that authorized users can no longer use the service in question. DDoS attacks are thus generally directed against the availability of services. During the Covid-19 pandemic, a very sharp increase in the number of DDoS attacks was observed. Figure 1 illustrates this statement with a comparison of the numbers before or during the beginning (2020) and during the peak of the pandemic (2021) for the example of Germany. Cloud services are accessed via the Internet, which is why DDoS attacks that specifically target cloud services or their providers are a tried-and-tested means of preventing the use of these services, at least temporarily.

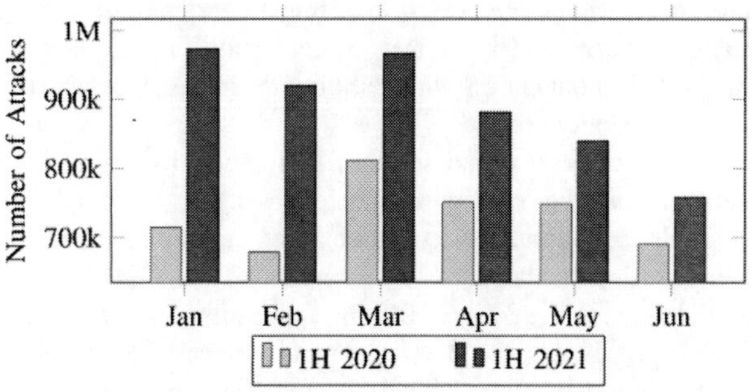

Figure 1. Monthly DDoS attack frequency during the Covid-19 pandemic in 2020 and 2021 (Germany) according to [13].

The current trends, as described in [14], are that adversary often using cloud-based Virtual Private Servers (VPS) to set up botnets that are used to execute DDoS attacks. This setup is much more powerful than botnets based on vulnerable IoT devices, which we have seen in recent years. The attack durations decrease but, on the other hand, ransom DDoS attacks are on the rise. In such an attack, the adversaries extort ransom payments from the victim by threatening – for example, after a brief demonstration of their capabilities – to launch further or longer DDoS attacks if the victim does not pay the demanded sum.

DDoS attacks may be prevented by using firewalls in combination with intrusion detection systems (IDS), traffic filtering and load balancing.

D. Dependence on 3rd Party Software

The complexity of modern cloud services usually means that hardly any provider develops the software required for the service completely in-house. Instead, it is common to fall back on established and tested libraries, etc., which are developed and provided by 3rd parties. In case of open source software, it is possible to critically examine the source code of this integrated software and analyzing it in terms of vulnerabilities. Unfortunately, very often people trust that this 3rd party software has been thoroughly tested and is secure without checking this further. Vulnerabilities due to programming errors or deficiencies in the software design cannot be ruled out, however, and are often only discovered when the software has already been in use for a long time. A well-known example of a vulnerability in 3rd party software is Log4Shell, which was given a CVSS severity rating of 10.0, the highest score possible [15]. Log4j is a Java-based logging utility which is used in open source and proprietary software alike and became a de facto standard for this purpose. The Log4Shell vulnerability allowed adversaries to remotely execute arbitrary code on the host system, e.g., to do some crypto mining on these systems. Quite a lot of services were affected, like Amazon Web Services (AWS) [16] or Apple's iCloud [17], for example.

In principle, it does not matter which functionality is realized by 3rd party software. But in practice these are often security features whose technical characteristics are often cloud-specific, but are generally not conceptually new. To put this in concrete terms, the implementation of security roles, authorization rules, key or certificate management and methods in connection with Public Key Infrastructures (PKI) may be mentioned.

The security of cloud services that use 3rd party software depends on the quality of such libraries, of course. For example, a vulnerability in an integrated authentication service can reveal personal data of customers of the CSP, which is a violation of the EU GDPR. In this example, it is initially irrelevant whether the data is generally accessible to anyone on the Internet (data breach) or whether getting access is much harder, but the data is stolen and published by an attacker. Responsible and liable in this case is the CSP, not the programmers of the (open source) library.

The use of 3rd party software always poses a certain risk. To minimize this, it is therefore advisable to check any 3rd party software very carefully for vulnerabilities and also to test it extensively in interaction with one's own software components.

E. Unsecured APIs

APIs (Application Programming Interfaces) play an important role in the communication between cloud services and applications. If APIs are not sufficiently secured, they may become a potential security vulnerability. For example, an unsecured interface in a cloud API could result in confidential data being accessible to anyone (cf. data breaches, Subsection II-A). Secure APIs are in the interest of all parties involved, regardless of whether others access one's own code or data via these interfaces or whether we use libraries provided by others via such APIs (cf. Subsection II-D).

A very good overview of security issues related to APIs is provided by the OWASP API Security Project [18]. They list the following security issues as their top 10:

1) Broken Object Level Authorization
2) Broken User Authentication
3) Excessive Data Exposure
4) Lack of Resources & Rate Limiting
5) Broken Function Level Authorization
6) Mass Assignment
7) Security Misconfiguration
8) Injection
9) Improper Assets Management
10) Insufficient Logging & Monitoring

Several of these issues have already been mentioned in this paper and all of the items speak for themselves for readers who are familiar with information security. At this point, however, it should be noted that all these mentioned security problems are explained in detail in the report cited and appropriate countermeasures are proposed as well. At the time of writing, the OWASP API Security Project is working on the 2023 version of their top 10 list.

F. Cloud-Native Security

The Kubernetes documentation [19] summarizes cloud-native security as "The 4C's of cloud Native security are cloud, Clusters, Containers, and Code". The first and most famous container engine, Docker, optimizes for developer experience and ease of use and explicitly not for security. The Docker daemon requires root privileges and is a single executable monolith with a wide attack surface. This leads to exploits like DirtyCOW, however, it is hard to understand clearly the principle of its underlying vulnerability of Linux operating system, even for experienced kernel developers [20].

Alternative container engines are available now, e.g. Podman, OpenStack KataContainers, AWS Firecracker, or Google gVisor. Many of them focus on security and provide, i.e., a rootless mode. Lize Rice provides an introduction into applied container security [21]. Amazon introduced the Shared Responsibility Model [22], which states that the provider is only responsible for security 'of' the cloud, while customers are responsible for security 'in' the cloud. The *10 Rules for Better Cloud Security* by GitGuardian [23] provide an entry point to measures that can be taken following the Shared Responsibility Model:

1) Don't overlook developer credentials (in public and private code repositories).
2) Always review default configurations.
3) List publicly accessible storage.
4) Regularly audit access control.
5) Leverage network constructs.
6) Make logging and monitoring preventive.
7) Enrich your asset inventory.

8) Prevent domain hijacking.
9) A disaster recovery plan is not optional!
10) Limit manual configurations.

Research about container security includes the creation of Trusted Execution Environments (TEE) for containers. Secure Linux containers can, e.g., be based on Intel SGX, as has been demonstrated by Arnautov et al. [24].

Finally, Kubernetes security is based on the 4Cs as mentioned above; all major CSPs provide guides to security and hardening of their Kubernetes environments [19]. Areas of concern for workload security in Kubernetes are, e.g., role-based access control (RBAC) authorization, application secrets management and encrypting them at rest, ensuring that pods meet defined pod security standards [25], and network policies.

III. Fog computing Security Challenges

Fog computing, a term coined by Cisco [26], is a distributed computing paradigm that bridges the gap between cloud computing and IoT devices. Rather than pushing all data to a remote cloud for processing, in fog computing, computations are instead carried out closer to the source of data – on the IoT devices themselves or on local edge servers. This minimizes the latency involved in long-distance data transport, optimizes system efficiency and improves real-time capabilities. By bringing computation and storage closer to the data sources, fog computing addresses issues like bandwidth constraints, latency, and security concerns that can be associated with cloud computing [27]. This approach is particularly beneficial for high mobility technologies like the IoT and Vehicular Ad-hoc Networks (VANETs), as it provides faster communication and software services to users. By reducing the distance between devices and computing resources, fog computing offers lower latency and improved quality of service compared to traditional cloud computing [2][28].

While fog computing shares some characteristics with cloud computing, it differs in several ways, such as balancing central and local computing, storage, and network management. This balance allows fog computing to offer more efficient, real-time control and improvements for various systems, including healthcare, traffic patterns, parking systems, and more. But, of course, fog computing is not without its challenges. Some of its limitations include lower resources compared to cloud computing, higher latency in certain cases, energy consumption concerns, load balancing, data management, and security threats [29].

Based on the afore mentioned characteristics, fog computing may be seen as an addition to traditional cloud computing. And in the context of this paper, these characteristics allow choosing between cloud or fog computing as a basis for specific ML applications or projects.

There are several security threats to fog computing that are comparable or similar to those to cloud computing. In general, fog computing involves a distributed network of devices, which increases the risk of network disruptions and downtime. So, besides data confidentiality, authenticity, and integrity, ensuring high availability is crucial to guarantee uninterrupted service delivery. Attacks can hinder the proper functioning of fog computing systems and may lead to unauthorized access, data leakage, or system failures [30]. To mitigate these attacks, fog computing systems must implement robust security measures, such as strong encryption, intrusion detection and prevention, access control, and continuous monitoring. Additionally, ensuring compliance with security standards and best practices can help minimize the risk of security breaches in fog computing environments [31]. A couple of security threats to fog computing have already been described in Section II. For example, DDoS attacks against fog computing networks aim to overwhelm fog nodes or networks with excessive traffic, causing disruptions and impacting services [32]. Additionally, there are other classical network attacks, like Man in the Middle (MITM) or replay attacks. A MITM attack in fog computing involves intercepting and manipulating communications between legitimate components, compromising the system's integrity, confidentiality, and availability [33]. A replay attack is a type of security threat where an adversary captures and retransmits previously exchanged messages between parties in a communication session, making it seem as if they are the legitimate sender [34]. In the context of fog computing, an adversary may impersonate end devices or the fog broker to carry out this attack. During a replay attack, the adversary neither needs to understand the content of the captured messages nor decrypt any encrypted data; they simply replay the messages to exploit the system. This could lead to various negative consequences, such as unauthorized access, data manipulation, or disruption of services.

In the following, we focus on threats and attacks that are more specific to fog than to cloud computing.

A. Physical Attacks

A physical attack in fog or edge computing [35] involves compromising the physical hardware of the system, such as servers or other devices. This can be particularly problematic in these systems because their infrastructure is distributed across various geographical locations. If the physical protection of these devices is inadequate, it could allow for tampering or damage. Since each device or server typically serves a local geographical area, any physical attack can disrupt services within that specific area. Hence, it's crucial to implement strong physical security measures alongside cybersecurity measures in fog computing.

B. Fog and User Impersonation Attack

This is a type of cyberattack where an adversary poses as another device or user on a network in order to launch attacks against network hosts, steal data, spread malware, or bypass access controls. This is a particularly insidious type of attack because it can be very difficult to detect, as the adversary is using credentials that are considered valid within the system. Impersonation attacks in fog computing can disrupt the communication between fog nodes and end devices, leading to miscommunication, data theft, or even disruption of service. As a countermeasure, Tu et al. suggest combining physical layer security techniques with a reinforcement learning algorithm to improve the security against impersonation attacks and optimize the decision-making process for distinguishing between legitimate and unauthorized entities [36].

C. Malicious Fog Nodes Attacks

A malicious fog node can compromise network operations through various attacks, affecting the reliability of fog-to-fog collaborations. Also, identifying malicious fog devices in fog computing is crucial. To prevent malicious fog node issues, organizations should implement a comprehensive security approach including authentication and authorization, data encryption, secure communication protocols, intrusion detection systems, trust management, regular monitoring, network segmentation, access control, and an incident response plan. These strategies help reduce risks, enhance overall security, and maintain system resilience. Consequently, achieving comprehensive protection against attacks becomes challenging, as it involves granting limited privileges and processing data. Finding appropriate countermeasures is the subject of current research, as examples we refer to Al-Khafajiy et al. [37] and Ke Gu et al. [38]. The latter present a fog computing-based VANET, in which a scheme is used to detect malicious nodes (vehicles or devices with harmful intent). In their approach, the fog server computes a reputation score for each potentially harmful node. This score is determined by examining the relationship between the data collected from the node and the overall network structure. By analyzing these factors, the fog server can more accurately identify and flag nodes that may pose a threat to the network's security and performance.

D. Rogue Fog Nodes

A rogue fog node attack is when a malicious node pretends to be a legitimate fog node and joins the network to perform attacks, such as eavesdropping, data theft, or denial of service [39].

To prevent rogue fog node attacks, the following measures can be taken:

- Authentication and authorization: Fog nodes should be authenticated and authorized before they are allowed to join the network. This can be achieved by implementing secure boot and mutual authentication mechanisms.
- Encryption: Sensitive data transmitted between fog nodes should be encrypted to prevent eavesdropping and data theft.
- Trust Management: Trust management protocols can be used to evaluate the trustworthiness of fog nodes. This can be based on the node's behavior, reputation, and credentials.
- Network Segmentation: Segmentation of the network can be used to isolate the fog nodes that are vulnerable to attacks. This can help in containing the attack and minimizing the damage.
- Continuous Monitoring: Continuous monitoring of the network can be used to detect any unauthorized fog node that joins the network. This can be achieved by monitoring network traffic, node behavior, and system logs.

E. Ephemeral Secret Leakage Attack

In the realm of fog computing, the Ephemeral Secret Leakage Attack [40] presents a notable risk due to the distributed architecture and sensitive data often involved. This attack, based on the Canetti-Krawczyk adversary model [41], assumes that an adversary can access one of the secret keys (short-term or long-term) used for secure communication between devices. If an adversary reveals a session key (a temporary encryption key), they can decipher all data exchanged during that session, leading to a potential security breach. Therefore, implementing robust cryptographic protocols and effective key management strategies is crucial for maintaining security in fog computing systems.

IV. Special Security Challenges for AI Applications

A. Data Representing ML models

Some of the previously mentioned attacks targeted data stored in the cloud or in a fog computing network. In addition to the consideration that this data is, for example, personal data of customers, which is then processed by the ML application, there is another relevant aspect. A crucial prerequisite for successful ML projects is very often a sufficiently large amount of training data. ML models are only as good as the quality of the training data. In many areas where ML methods have not yet been applied or in the case of new business models, no training data are available at the beginning. These often have to be created laboriously at first, which on the one hand may mean a large number of measurements to generate a sufficiently large sample set and on the other hand often means the manual labeling of the training data. Against the background of the threats and attacks discussed earlier, it should therefore be emphasized that ML models and their training data are very valuable assets. Unavailable models or training data due to a DDoS attack can lead to severe business interruptions. But even worse would be if models or training data that are exposed on the Internet or stolen fall into the hands of a competitor. This could even spell the end for a company whose business model is based on such ML projects.

B. Special AI-Related Security Issues

The special situation arising when working with AI algorithms is the way the models are trained, deployed, integrated and used in industrial environments (cf. Figure 2).

Typically, the models are centrally trained on special high performance computers or servers and after training and evaluation transferred to the application server. Referring to Figure 2, Step A, the data scientist and co-workers create the data set extracted from typical information sources such as sensors, databases and image archives. In Step B, the data set is checked for validity, activities such as annotation (class assignment), feature extraction and the integration of domain-specific additional knowledge expand the data set in this step.

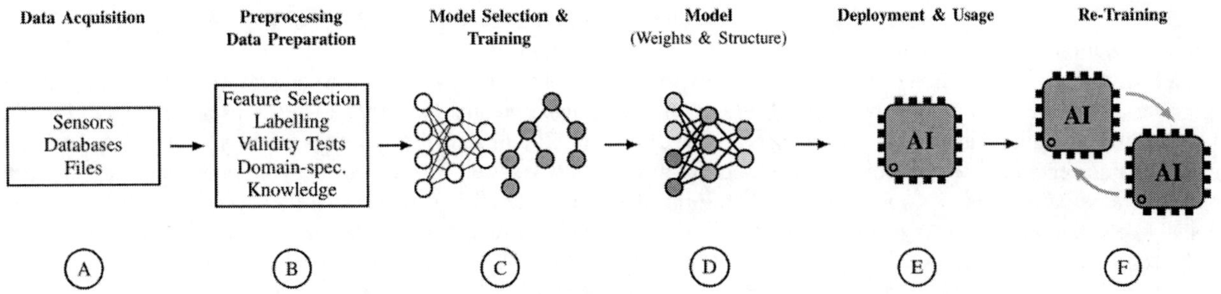

Figure 2. Typical AI workflow in different steps (A to F). Note: The deployment and application steps typically run on different systems.

Next, various models and AI architectures are applied to the data set and are then evaluated in Step C. Usually, the approach/model with the highest robustness and accuracy is used and deployed. Depending on the data set, the time needed to train a model can vary between minutes or several days on high performance computers. Step D addresses the fully trained model. The parameters of the model represent possible clusters or class memberships (the *intelligence*). Step E covers the deployment and application of the model. This includes the data preparation steps in the production environment, feature calculation and forward propagation of the feature vector in the AI model. The application runs on an application server, which usually requires a different level of security. A detached Step F is the re-training of the AI model: new aspects that have arisen either through extension of the use case or through additional data during operation must be integrated into the model. Usually, not the entire system is re-trained, but parts of the upper layers of a network are algorithmically adapted.

We now consider the workflow shown in Figure 2 against the background of an industrial application, for example in a modern production line. Concerning the security of the AI model, three different scenarios can occur. In the **poisoned data set** scenario, the adversary, e.g. a malicious insider, has inserted harmful information into the data set that does not match the desired class and thus negatively influences and disrupts the AI structure after the training process. In general, ML poisoning attacks refer to the manipulation of data used for the (re-)training of ML models, e.g., in a fog environment [42]. Especially in edge systems, basic AI training is performed at a central processing system due to the lack of processing resources. The generalized model is then deployed on the edge system and adapted to the application requirements using smaller local data sets or calibration steps. This local adaption process is prone to attacks as the training data is locally gathered without any supervision by experts.

To prevent ML poisoning attacks, here are some countermeasures that can be taken:

- **Use of Secure Data Sources**: Data sources must be secure and access to them should be restricted to authorized personnel only. It must be possible to check and verify the validity of the data at any time.
- **Data Sanitization**: The data should be checked and cleaned before it is used to train ML models. Any data that is found to be suspicious or anomalous should be removed. It may not be possible to automate this, but must be done manually.
- **Anomaly Detection**: Anomaly detection techniques can be used to detect any malicious data in the training data set. AI-based anomaly detection based on autoencoders, recurrent neural networks (RNN) or generative adversarial networks (GAN) can be considered as state of the art.
- **Ensemble Learning**: Ensemble learning is a technique where multiple ML models are trained on different subsets of the data. This can make it harder for adversaries to manipulate the data in order to affect the overall prediction.
- **Continuous Monitoring**: Continuous monitoring of the ML model's behavior is essential to detect any unusual or unexpected outcomes. Any anomalies should be investigated and addressed promptly.

In the **compromised AI model** scenario, the adversary changes the trained weights (parameters) of the AI network which leads to falsified outputs (cf. Step D). Therefore, security measures to ensure the integrity of the data must be used in order to prevent manipulation. Of course, these measures must not interfere with the re-training of the model (cf. Step F). It is conceivable to switch off these measures during re-training, but this requires that re-training is thoroughly monitored and secured against unauthorized access. If this is not possible or does not make sense, e.g., because the re-training is automated, a trust management system should be considered that evaluates the trustworthiness of the data for re-training and detects manipulated model parameters.

The third scenario addresses deployment, integration and utilization of the AI system in the production environment (cf. Step E). Information **inputs and results of the AI network** might as well be compromised: Either false/noisy information is presented to the network (input, e.g. by manipulated sensors) or the results are falsified and thus passed on incorrectly. In both cases, this interferes with the production steps that follow. Statistical analysis of the production can detect these kind of attacks.

The above-mentioned security precautions can be introduced at various points in the processing architecture. In a fog environment, for instance, edge systems act as supervisors for local information sources; status information forwarded from edge nodes to central units must be checked and validated before integration into central data sets.

In addition to the organizational challenges in the use of AI algorithms, there are also semantic problems: If habits change in the application field, this leads to sudden changes that trigger anomaly detection. Low-threshold changes, such as those applied by adversaries in the network area, may undermine the anomaly detection process. It is therefore necessary to weigh up the sensitivity of such approaches.

C. Special Attacks on Language Models

In this subsection, we focus on special attacks on language models.

Suppose an attacker has access to multiple snapshots of an ML model, such as predictive keyboards. Then these snapshots can reveal detailed information about the change in training data used to update the model. This is called a model update attack. Zanella-Béguelin et al. analyzed information leakage in practical applications where language models are frequently updated, for example, by adding new data, deleting user data to meet privacy requirements, or matching private data with that of public, pre-trained language models. They developed two new metrics to analyze the information leakage, which now enables them to perform this kind of leakage analysis unsupervised [43].

Tab attacks are attacks on language models that rely on autocompletion and in which the adversary attempts to cause the model to provide unwanted suggestions or results. So, these attacks target text recognition systems or try to figure out the robustness of language models. This involves an attempt to intentionally deceive the language model by deliberately inserting false or misleading information or creating distortions in the input data. Large language models are capable of memorizing rare training samples, which poses serious privacy threats in case the model is trained on confidential user content. Inan et al. have developed a methodology for checking a language model for training data leaks. This enables the creator of the model to determine to what extent training examples can be extracted from the model in a practical attack. And the owner of the model is able to verify that deployed countermeasures work as expected, and thus that their model can be used securely [44].

V. Conclusion and Future Work

In this paper, we have illustrated the dependency of AI applications on underlying cloud or fog-based services. Attacks against the cloud services or fog computing networks on which current AI applications are built will inevitably result in difficulties, data breaches, failures, or malfunctioning of the AI applications. AI is one of the current hot topics, resulting in high demand for related services. This makes them an attractive target for cybercriminals: they can try to prevent access to AI services on the Internet in order to extort a ransom from the service provider; they can also try to steal training data or complete ML models in order to have the owners pay for getting their data back or sell them to others, e.g., to competitors, at the highest bid.

The interplay between AI and information security promises huge potential for future applications and research. For example, this paper did not even address how AI methods could also be used in order to support threat analysis of systems or penetration testing. It is already possible to use language models to generate phishing emails optimized for a specific target. Due to this huge potential of the interaction of AI and information security, we intend to continue to be active in these areas in the future.

References

[1] D. K. Sharma *et al.*, "Cloud computing in medicine: Current trends and possibilities," in *2021 International Conference on Advancements in Electrical, Electronics, Communication, Computing and Automation (ICAECA)*, IEEE, 2021, pp. 1–5.

[2] A. V. Dastjerdi, H. Gupta, R. N. Calheiros, S. K. Ghosh, and R. Buyya, "Fog computing: Principles, architectures, and applications," in *Internet of Things: Principles and Paradigms*, R. Buyya and A. V. Dastjerdi, Eds., Morgan Kaufmann, 2016, pp. 61–75.

[3] National Security Agency, "Cybersecurity information – cloud security basics," National Security Agency, Aug. 29, 2018. [Online]. Available: https://www.nsa.gov/portals/75/documents/what-we-do/cybersecurity/professional-resources/csi-cloud-security-basics.pdf (visited on 06/08/2023).

[4] F. Süß, M. Freimuth, A. Aßmuth, G. Weir, and R. Duncan, "Cloud security and security challenges revisited," in *Proceedings of Cloud Computing 2019*, B. Duncan, Y. W. Lee, M. Westerlund, and A. Aßmuth, Eds., IARIA, May 2019, pp. 61–66.

[5] R. Barona and E. A. M. Anita, "A survey on data breach challenges in cloud computing security: Issues and threats," in *2017 International Conference on Circuit ,Power and Computing Technologies (ICCPCT)*, 2017, pp. 1–8. DOI: 10.1109/ICCPCT.2017.8074287.

[6] F. Sabahi, "Cloud computing security threats and responses," in *2011 IEEE 3rd International Conference on Communication Software and Networks*, 2011, pp. 245–249. DOI: 10.1109/ICCSN.2011.6014715.

[7] M. Henriquez, "The top data breaches of 2021," Security Magazine, Dec. 9, 2021, [Online]. Available: https://www.securitymagazine.com/articles/96667-the-top-data-breaches-of-2021 (visited on 06/08/2023).

[8] J. Fitzgerald, "The 10 biggest data breaches of 2022," CRN Security News, Dec. 28, 2022, [Online]. Available: https://www.crn.com/news/security/the-10-biggest-data-breaches-of-2022 (visited on 06/08/2023).

[9] Admin, "The 25 biggest data breaches and attacks of 2020," StealthLabs, Dec. 16, 2020, [Online]. Available: https://www.stealthlabs.com/blog/the-25-biggest-data-breaches-and-attacks-of-2020/ (visited on 06/08/2023).

[10] D. Cameron, "Today's massive ransomware attack was mostly preventable; here's how to avoid it," Gizmodo, May 13, 2017, [Online]. Available: https://www.gizmodo.com.au/2017/05/todays-massive-ransomware-attack-was-mostly-preventable-heres-how-to-avoid-it/ (visited on 06/08/2023).

[11] M. R. Watson, N.-h. Shirazi, A. K. Marnerides, A. Mauthe, and D. Hutchison, "Malware detection in cloud computing infrastructures," *IEEE Transactions on Dependable and Secure Computing*, vol. 13, no. 2, pp. 192–205, 2016. DOI: 10.1109/TDSC.2015.2457918.

[12] A. K. Kibet, R. A. Esquivel, and J. A. Esquivel, "Ransomware: Ransomware as a service (raas), methods to detects, prevent, mitigate and future directions," *Journal of Emerging Technologies and Innovative Research*, vol. 9, no. 11, b264–b278, 2022.

[13] Netscout, "Threat intelligence report, issue 7: Findings from 1h 2021," Netscout, Tech. Rep. p. 7, 2021.

[14] O. Yoachimik and J. Pacheco, "Ddos threat report for 2023 q1," Cloudflare, Apr. 11, 2023, [Online]. Available: https://blog.cloudflare.com/ddos-threat-report-2023-q1/ (visited on 06/08/2023).

[15] National Vulnerability Database, "Cve-2021-44228 detail," National Institute of Standards and Technology, Dec. 10, 2021, [Online]. Available: https://nvd.nist.gov/vuln/detail/CVE-2021-44228 (visited on 06/08/2023).

[16] D. Nalley and V. Simonis, "Hotpatch for apache log4j," AWS Open Source Blog, Dec. 12, 2021, [Online]. Available: https://aws.amazon.com/blogs/opensource/hotpatch-for-apache-log4j/ (visited on 06/08/2023).

[17] hoakley, "Last week on my mac: When the internet caught fire," The Eclectic Light Company, Dec. 12, 2021, [Online]. Available: https://eclecticlight.co/2021/12/12/last-week-on-my-mac-when-the-internet-caught-fire/ (visited on 06/08/2023).

[18] E. Yalon, I. Shkedy, and P. Silva, "Owasp api security top 2019," Open Worldwide Application Security Project, 2019, [Online]. Available: https://owasp.org/www-project-api-security/ (visited on 06/08/2023).

[19] Kubernetes, "Overview of Cloud Native Security," Sep. 2022, [Online]. Available: https://kubernetes.io/docs/concepts/security/overview/ (visited on 06/08/2023).

[20] Y. Wen and J. Wang, "Analysis and remodeling of the DirtyCOW vulnerability by debugging and abstraction," in *Structured Object-Oriented Formal Language and Method: 9th International Workshop (SOFL+ MSVL) 2019, Shenzhen, China*, Springer, 2020, pp. 3–12.

[21] L. Rice, *Container security: Fundamental technology concepts that protect containerized applications*. O'Reilly, 2020.

[22] Amazon, "Shared Responsibility Model," 2015, [Online]. Available: https://aws.amazon.com/en/compliance/shared-responsibility-model/ (visited on 06/08/2023).

[23] T. Segura, "10 Rules for Better Cloud Security," Dec. 2021, [Online]. Available: https://blog.gitguardian.com/10-rules-for-better-cloud-security/ (visited on 06/08/2023).

[24] S. Arnautov *et al.*, "SCONE: Secure linux containers with intel SGX," in *12th USENIX Symposium on Operating Systems Design and Implementation (OSDI '16)*, vol. 16, 2016, pp. 689–703.

[25] GitGuardian, "Kubernetes hardening tutorial part 1: Pods," Dec. 2021, [Online]. Available: https://blog.gitguardian.com/kubernetes-tutorial-part-1-pods/ (visited on 06/08/2023).

[26] Cisco Systems, Inc., "Fog computing and the internet of things: Extend the cloud to where the things are," Cisco Systems, Inc., Tech. Rep. C11-734435-00, 2015.

[27] F. Bonomi, R. Milito, J. Zhu, and S. Addepalli, "Fog computing and its role in the internet of things," in *Proceedings of the First Edition of the MCC Workshop on Mobile Cloud Computing*, ser. MCC '12, Helsinki, Finland: Association for Computing Machinery, 2012, pp. 13–16, ISBN: 9781450315197. DOI: 10.1145/2342509.2342513. [Online]. Available: https://doi.org/10.1145/2342509.2342513.

[28] R. Mahmud, R. Kotagiri, and R. Buyya, "Fog computing: A taxonomy, survey and future directions," in *Internet of Things*, Springer Singapore, Oct. 2017, pp. 103–130. DOI: 10.1007/978-981-10-5861-5_5. [Online]. Available: https://doi.org/10.1007/978-981-10-5861-5_5.

[29] Cisco Systems, Inc., "Cisco fog computing solutions: Unleash the power of the internet of things," Cisco Systems, Inc., Tech. Rep. C11-734589-00, 2015.

[30] S. Khan, S. Parkinson, and Y. Qin, "Fog computing security: A review of current applications and security solutions," *Journal of Cloud Computing*, vol. 6, no. 1, pp. 1–22, Aug. 2017. DOI: 10.1186/s13677-017-0090-3. [Online]. Available: https://doi.org/10.1186/s13677-017-0090-3.

[31] A. Aljumah and T. A. Ahanger, "Fog computing and security issues: A review," in *2018 7th International Conference on Computers Communications and Control (ICCCC)*, 2018, pp. 237–239. DOI: 10.1109/ICCCC.2018.8390464.

[32] M. Mukherjee *et al.*, "Security and privacy in fog computing: Challenges," *IEEE Access*, vol. 5, pp. 19293–19304, 2017. DOI: 10.1109/ACCESS.2017.2749422.

[33] F. Aliyu, T. Sheltami, and E. M. Shakshuki, "A detection and prevention technique for man in the middle attack in fog computing," *Procedia Computer Science*, vol. 141, pp. 24–31, 2018, The 9th International Conference on Emerging Ubiquitous Systems and Pervasive Networks (EUSPN-2018) / The 8th International Conference on Current and Future Trends of Information and Communication Technologies in Healthcare (ICTH-2018) / Affiliated Workshops, ISSN: 1877-0509. DOI: https://doi.org/10.1016/j.procs.2018.10.125. [Online]. Available: https://www.sciencedirect.com/science/article/pii/S1877050918317733.

[34] M. Hosseinzadeh, B. Sinopoli, and E. Garone, "Feasibility and detection of replay attack in networked constrained cyber-physical systems," in *2019 57th Annual Allerton Conference on Communication, Control, and Computing (Allerton)*, 2019, pp. 712–717. DOI: 10.1109/ALLERTON.2019.8919762.

[35] A. M. Alwakeel, "An overview of fog computing and edge computing security and privacy issues," *Sensors*, vol. 21, no. 24, p. 8226, Dec. 2021. DOI: 10.3390/s21248226. [Online]. Available: https://doi.org/10.3390/s21248226.

[36] S. Tu *et al.*, "Security in fog computing: A novel technique to tackle an impersonation attack," *IEEE Access*, vol. 6, pp. 74993–75001, 2018. DOI: 10.1109/ACCESS.2018.2884672.

[37] M. Al-khafajiy *et al.*, "COMITMENT: A fog computing trust management approach," *Journal of Parallel and Distributed Computing*, vol. 137, pp. 1–16, Mar. 2020. DOI: 10.1016/j.jpdc.2019.10.006. [Online]. Available: https://doi.org/10.1016/j.jpdc.2019.10.006.

[38] K. Gu, X. Dong, and W. Jia, "Malicious node detection scheme based on correlation of data and network topology in fog computing-based vanets," *IEEE Transactions on Cloud Computing*, vol. 10, no. 2, pp. 1215–1232, 2022. DOI: 10.1109/TCC.2020.2985050.

[39] S. Yi, Z. Qin, and Q. Li, "Security and privacy issues of fog computing: A survey," in *Wireless Algorithms, Systems, and Applications*, K. Xu and H. Zhu, Eds., Cham: Springer International Publishing, 2015, pp. 685–695, ISBN: 978-3-319-21837-3.

[40] F. Dewanta, "Secure microservices deployment for fog computing services in a remote office," in *2020 3rd International Conference on Information and Communications Technology (ICOIACT)*, 2020, pp. 425–430. DOI: 10.1109/ICOIACT50329.2020.9332025.

[41] R. Canetti and H. Krawczyk, "Analysis of key-exchange protocols and their use for building secure channels," in *Advances in Cryptology — EUROCRYPT 2001*, B. Pfitzmann, Ed., Berlin, Heidelberg: Springer Berlin Heidelberg, 2001, pp. 453–474, ISBN: 978-3-540-44987-4.

[42] Y. Qi, M. S. Hossain, J. Nie, and X. Li, "Privacy-preserving blockchain-based federated learning for traffic flow prediction," *Future Generation Computer Systems*, vol. 117, pp. 328–337, 2021, ISSN: 0167-739X. DOI: https://doi.org/10.1016/j.future.2020.12.003. [Online]. Available: https://www.sciencedirect.com/science/article/pii/S0167739X2033065X.

[43] S. Zanella-Béguelin *et al.*, "Analyzing information leakage of updates to natural language models," in *ACM Conference on Computer and Communication Security (CCS)*, ACM, ACM, 2020. [Online]. Available: https://www.microsoft.com/en-us/research/publication/analyzing-information-leakage-of-updates-to-natural-language-models/.

[44] H. A. Inan *et al.*, *Training data leakage analysis in language models*, 2021. DOI: 10.48550/ARXIV.2101.05405. [Online]. Available: https://arxiv.org/abs/2101.05405.

On the Creation of a Secure Key Enclave via the Use of Memory Isolation in Systems Management Mode

James Andrew Sutherland, Natalie Coull & Robert Ian Ferguson
Division of Cybersecurity
Abertay University
Dundee, UK
email: {j.sutherland, n.coull, ian.ferguson}@abertay.ac.uk

Abstract — **One of the challenges of modern cloud computer security is how to isolate or contain data and applications in a variety of ways, while still allowing sharing where desirable. Hardware-based attacks such as RowHammer and Spectre have demonstrated the need to safeguard the cryptographic operations and keys from tampering upon which so much current security technology depends. This paper describes research into security mechanisms for protecting sensitive areas of memory from tampering or intrusion using the facilities of Systems Management Mode. The work focuses on the creation of a small, dedicated area of memory in which to perform cryptographic operations, isolated from the rest of the system. The approach has been experimentally validated by a case study involving the creation of a secure webserver whose encryption key is protected using this approach such that even an intruder with full Administrator level access cannot extract the key.**

Keywords- key-enclave; hardware security; system-management mode.

I. INTRODUCTION

Computer security is largely concerned with erecting boundaries between entities: users, privilege levels, processes. Wherever a resource crosses a boundary, it creates the potential for compromise, either through passive information leakage (as in the case of timing attacks, where the exact details of how long an operation takes inadvertently discloses some information) or the potential for active tampering (as in RowHammer [1], where writing to one memory location indirectly affects another through non-obvious electrical coupling between parts of a memory chip).

A. Motivation

Attacks based upon covert channels and side channels depend on unexpected interactions; RowHammer for example, can be used to achieve privilege escalation via a previously-unexpected interaction between physically proximate memory components [2] . Since there was no correlation between physical and virtual addresses, as different processes and the kernel would commingle pages arbitrarily, low-privilege pages could easily be found which happened to be adjacent to highly sensitive system ones, allowing tampering. The same applies between virtual machines and hypervisor control structures. As detailed later, the more coarse-grained the sharing gets, the more limited the avenues of attack become, though any level of shared caching can be an avenue of attack [3].

As encryption keys are typically stored in RAM, a successful compromise of a system via techniques such as these can reveal those keys used to protect data at rest on the system, e.g., full-disk encryption, and data in transit to/from the system, e.g., via an SSL connection.

The ability to improve segregation of memory to securely store keys etc. separately from less sensitive data has previously required a system to have dedicated features, e.g., Intel's SGX integrated with the processor. The consequences of an attack that compromises such facilities can be widespread: In the case of SGX, this protection was defeated in 2018 via side-channel attack [4], forcing Intel to update SGX's deployment mechanism to be able to check whether the Spectre [5] attacks were properly mitigated on the target hardware.

B. An alternative approach to creating an enclave

The current generation of Intel processor architectures have a feature called Systems Management Mode (SMM) which can be used during the boot process to create an area of RAM (SMRAM), which is subsequently 'locked' and thus rendered inaccessible/unusable by 'userland' code. This offers the possibility of creating a secure memory enclave for the storage of cryptographic keys and the code which manipulates them (negotiation, verification etc.) The locked area can only be accessed by returning to SMM mode which automatically executes the code that has been securely locked in that area. This fact led to the following research hypothesis for the work:

Secure isolation can be practically implemented using only the long-established Systems Management Mode mechanisms, giving better security isolation than existing techniques such as process separation.

The work described in the remainder of this paper shows how this can be used to create a secure enclave. It is worth noting that some other processor architectures, e.g., ARM, have equivalent facilities and the proposed technique for enclave creation is thus generalisable.

The material in the paper is based on the PhD thesis of the first author and is published here for the first time [6].

The remainder of the paper is structured thus: In Section II previous work on providing secure key stores is considered. This acts as a baseline for comparison with the technique presented here. Section III describes the proposed solution to this problem whilst Section IV discusses how the approach was evaluated. The results of the evaluation are given in Section V. Conclusions and proposals for further developing the approach are given in Section VI.

II. BACKGROUND

The provision of cryptographic services to a system depends upon the inviolability of any stored keys. As such services form the basis of secure computing, a secure place to store them is referred to as a Trusted Computing Base (TCB). Finding a means of creating such a TCB in RAM is thus an important security problem. This section therefore reviews various attempts at organising and protecting memory, dating from early multi-tasking operating systems and the consequent need to provide process separation through to recent hardware crypto-key enclaves before going on to review the solution-space technique of System Management Mode.

A. Protecting memory

1) Memory management/virtual memory

The idea of programs sharing system resources without interfering with each other can be traced back to the MIT 'Compatible Time Sharing System' [7]. Prior to this, only one process would be executing hence the idea of 'interference' did not apply.

Modern processor architectures implement some form of virtual memory mapping [8]: the memory a user process can access at address 0x10000, for example, may be stored in any arbitrary page of physical memory, or indeed be entirely absent and filled in by the operating system when an attempt is next made to access that, known as a 'page fault'.

To reduce the overhead of loading this mapping from memory, processors generally feature Translation Lookaside Buffers (TLBs), a set of cached address mappings. (Architectures have varying approaches to this; on MIPS, the operating system explicitly populates TLB entries as needed; x86 and more recent ARM variants populate TLB entries directly within the hardware without OS involvement, while the original ARMv2 had 512 explicit memory mappings within the MEMC1 memory controller chip as Content Addressable Memory.)

A key concept in ensuring that concurrently executing programs cannot interfere with each other or access their data is that each process be allocated its own set of memory pages and be unable to access RAM outwith those bounds. Attacks such as RowHammer, Heartbleed [9] and Spectre have shown that such OS-enforced restrictions can be circumvented and thus a more secure approach is required when storing particularly sensitive information such as encryption keys.

2) RAM Encryption

TRESOR [10] demonstrated that a general-purpose computer system can be operated with almost all of its main-memory encrypted while at rest, albeit with a significant performance penalty, using a modified Linux kernel. There is some overlap with the research this paper describes: TRESOR uses the processor debug registers as an area of storage which cannot be accessed via Direct Memory Access (DMA). This was intended to protect against DMA attacks, among others, but was not successful in that respect since this cannot protect the associated code: TRESOR-Hunt [11] demonstrated a successful attack on this protection, using code injection via DMA - an attack which could not be prevented through software mechanisms alone.

TreVisor [12] extended the techniques of TRESOR to a hypervisor level in combination with techniques from BitVisor [13] to incorporate Intel VT-d (IOMMU) protection from DMA attack.

On other platforms, the ARMORED [14] project applied TRESOR techniques to the Android operating system on ARM architecture processors as a countermeasure to their own FROST [15] attack, which used a cold boot attack to retrieve information from mobile handsets running Android 4.0 despite the disk encryption employed.

3) Address Space Layout Randomisation - ASLR

Traditionally software systems (and operating systems in particular) locate certain critical pieces of information at well-known, or at least predictable, memory addresses. Having its origins in the (Linux) PaX project [16] ASLR involves varying the location of memory contents over time thus making it more difficult for an attacker to find those critical locations.

4) Swap encryption

A cold boot attack can retrieve RAM contents for a brief period after a system is shut down, but the system's virtual memory persists indefinitely after shutdown unless explicitly wiped. To avoid this, keeping that data encrypted is an idea which long predates efforts to encrypt or otherwise protect the RAM, including the encrypted swap space [17] extensions to the virtual memory (VM) system originally proposed as an enhancement of the original 4.4 BSD approach [7]. The much slower nature of disk storage meant the extra overhead of this encryption was more widely accepted early on.

B. Other approaches to key protection

The approaches outlined above are general in that they seek to prevent cross-process interference between any two processes. Given the sensitive nature of crypto-services/keys, i.e. the consequences of their compromise, work has been done specifically on preventing inappropriate access to such keys: This sub-section reviews some typical attempts to provide such an enclave.

1) Process separation

Process separation in a cryptographic context is a software system design principle that demands that all handling of keys and cryptographic operations be performed in a separate process from the 'worker' process thus relying on the properties of the OS memory management system to deny the 'worker' any access to sensitive information. Its importance to the current work that the performance of our SSM-based solution is compared with a 'process separation' solution in experiment 4b (See Section IV).

2) Process isolation

The commercial content delivery network (CDN) Cloudflare has an interesting implementation of TLS/SSL in two respects. First, they offer 'Keyless SSL' [18] in which the site's private key is handled remotely. Secondly, the

SSL/TLS handling is performed in a separate isolated instance of the Nginx web server — an example of defence in depth which ensured that when a bug was found in their HTML parsing implementation, the information disclosed could not include site private keys, unlike with the widespread Heartbleed bug in OpenSSL [19] — only a kernel or hardware level exploit could have exposed the key, not an application level one.

3) VM isolation/hypervisors

Microsoft recently released a software-only implementation of a similar approach, Credential Guard [20], in which authentication keys are held in a dedicated virtual machine running on top of the Hyper-V hypervisor platform. This way, even a kernel compromise of the main operating system is not sufficient to extract credentials for reuse: no more 'Pass The Hash' privilege escalation once a system is compromised. Only a compromise of the underlying hypervisor itself, or the hardware isolation mechanisms, would suffice: a much smaller attack surface compared to the full OS.

4) Trusted Platform Module

The primary alternative to the general approach outlined above, where enhanced security is needed compared to direct key handling without extra isolation, is to use a dedicated cryptographic hardware device. Some PCs and servers are now equipped with a Trusted Platform Module (TPM) which provides a dedicated cryptographic and storage facility, with a fixed set of algorithms, limited storage and minimal performance [21].

5) Intel Software Guard Extensions - SGX

Intel Software Guard Extensions aim to deliver similar benefits within the main processor through architectural extensions, with an encrypted area of main memory rather than one isolated by the memory controller hardware. SGX-Shield [22] reviews the main limitations of this implementation and proposes an implementation of ASLR (varying the location of memory contents to make attacks more difficult) within this enclave for additional protection from outside interference.

This isolation is a mixed blessing, providing a hiding place for less benign code as well [23], while failing to protect against variants of the Spectre attack [4]. The TaLoS project [24] has significant similarities to the final experiment in Section V, in that it seeks to protect the encryption keys and traffic over an SSL/TLS connection but using SGX rather than SMM to isolate the data in question.

C. System Management Mode (SMM)

The approach considered in this paper is based upon the System Management Mode of the x86 family of processors (see Figure 1). As its operation provides the security guarantees necessary for creating a key enclave, it is discussed here in detail.

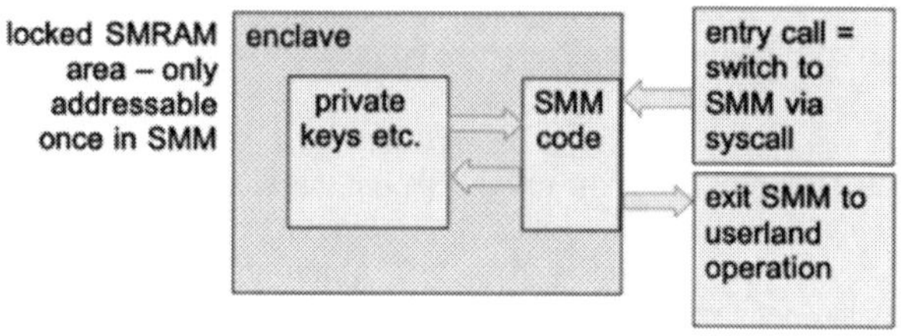

Figure 1. System Management Mode

The defining characteristic of SMM is that while the processor core is executing code in that mode, it asserts the SMIACT2 output line. This signal is interpreted by the Memory Controller Hub (MCH): when asserted, addresses are decoded differently, enabling access to the otherwise-inaccessible SMRAM area. Physically, this is just part of the main RAM, but gated by the memory controller to prevent non-SMM access. In early SMM implementations, the address used was 0xA0000, which is also used by legacy graphics support: any attempt by non-SMM code to read or write this area will access the video memory instead.

The location of SMRAM is defined by the SMBASE register, initially set to 0x30000 (192 kilobytes from the bottom of the memory space); setting the G_SMRAME control flag on the processor's SMRAMC (SMRAM control) register puts 128 kilobytes of SMRAM at a base address of 0xA0000, or 640 kilobytes, while setting T_EN (TSEG Enable) grants access to a larger area higher up. The address layout is depicted in Table I.

TABLE I. THE X86 PROCESSOR MEMORY MAP

Address	Size	Content (normal)	Content (SMM)
0xF0000	64k	BIOS ROM	
0xC0000	192k	Device ROM/Upper Memory Blocks	
0xA0000	128k	Legacy video	SMRAM
0x00000	640k	Legacy (DOS) memory	

It is important to note that SMM is not a privileged mode of execution as such, despite common references to it as 'ring -1' or 'ring -2' as if it were a more privileged alternative to ring 0 in which kernel code executes. For example, Wojtczuk and Rutkowska [25] refers to "escalation from ring 3 to SMM" — in reality, SMM code is entered in ring 0, and can transition to a reduced privilege level if desired.

In all cases, access to the SMRAM area is permitted only if the access is by the processor core (as opposed to any other peripheral), and then only if either SMIACT is asserted or the D_OPEN control bit in the system chipset is set to permit this. As a result, SMRAM has robust protection against any sort of DMA attack: attempted access from the PCI bus or elsewhere is not valid at any time.

1) Bootstrapping SMM

As noted earlier, access to the dedicated area of memory SMM uses (the SMRAM) is gated by the memory controller. In order to bootstrap the SMI handler, however, it must be possible to load this memory area before the first SMI instance. This is permitted by the D_OPEN control bit in the chipset: when set, this bit permits access to SMRAM without being in SMM. After initialisation is complete, this bit should be cleared and the D_LCK (Lock) bit set, rendering all the SMM control registers read-only until the processor is reset.

This should be done very early in the system boot process by the system BIOS before activating any peripherals or executing any other code to prevent malicious code using SMM as a hiding place; older BIOS implementations often failed to secure the state properly during the boot process, leaving the way open for a variety of SMM rootkits at least as far back as 2009 [26].

2) Using SMM for security

Soon after malicious use of SMM's isolation property was demonstrated, more benign uses were found, with HyperGuard [27] in 2008, HyperCheck [28] in 2010, HyperVerify [29] in 2013 and a US patent on the concept being granted in 2014 [30].

The TrustZone-based Real-time Kernel Protection (TZ-RKP) [31] applies the same concepts to an ARM system, using ARM's TrustZone mechanism in place of SMM. (TrustZone was created later, with a 'Secure World' entered by invoking a Secure Monitor Call exception.)

The underlying concept in each case is to generate then periodically verify cryptographic hashes of critical structures or code, in HyperGuard's case, by walking the Page Tables to identify all executable pages marked for supervisor access. At the time, this was not wholly sufficient since the processor could still execute non-supervisor pages with supervisor privilege; the later development of Supervisor Mode Execution Protection (SMEP) by Intel [32] closed this loophole.

The level of privilege at which code executes in x86 Protected Mode is determined by the two least significant bits of the CS (Code Selector/Segment) register, so the code at a single address in memory may normally be executed at any privilege level without modification. This has its origins in the 80286's implementation of Protected Mode, prior to the 80386's introduction of paged virtual memory: as the two mechanisms were orthogonal, prior to SMEP a page could be user writable (ring 3) yet run at kernel privilege (ring 0).

III. PROPOSED SOLUTION

This work aims to secure a network-connected system against remote or transient physical attack, using a simple web server as the model and endeavouring to protect it against unauthorised information disclosure, in particular, disclosure of the cryptographic keys which are used to authenticate the server to clients. The keys and the code used to negotiate and verify them are protected by storing them in SMRAM as outlined in the previous section. The approach is clearly generalisable to securing the authentication material on the client end as well: client cryptographic keys, stored passwords, and payment mechanisms could also be improved. This section thus describes how a secure proof-of-concept webserver was created which uses an SMM enclave to protect the keys it uses for serving HTTPS requests.

The starting point in creating the proof-of-concept server was an OpenSSL example TLS server [33] which was linked with Google's SSL implementation: BoringSSL [34] to which was added code implementing the SMM key protection from the previous section. The server runs as a normal unprivileged application ('ring 3') under Linux and used TLS 1.2.

Key design goals for the proof-of-concept server were a minimal overhead in each transition to/from SMM, and presenting a minimal attack surface on the SMM component while enabling the application counterpart to run with minimal privileges. From the programmer's perspective, the enclave functions in a manner akin to a physical hardware device, passing messages in both directions via a page of physical memory.

A. Overall operation

Three actions are necessary at boot time:

- A public/private key pair are generated (see Section III.A.1 "Key Negotiation" below)
- The private key and the code for verifying a candidate public key are placed in the SMRAM page.
- The SMRAM is locked (using technique described in Section II.C.1)

In subsequent operations, i.e., when the webserver wishes to serve a page, there is a need to pass information to the code now locked in SMRAM. This is achieved through the use of a small (4Kb) area (known as the 'mailslot') which is accessible from both inside and outside of SMM (See Figure 2).

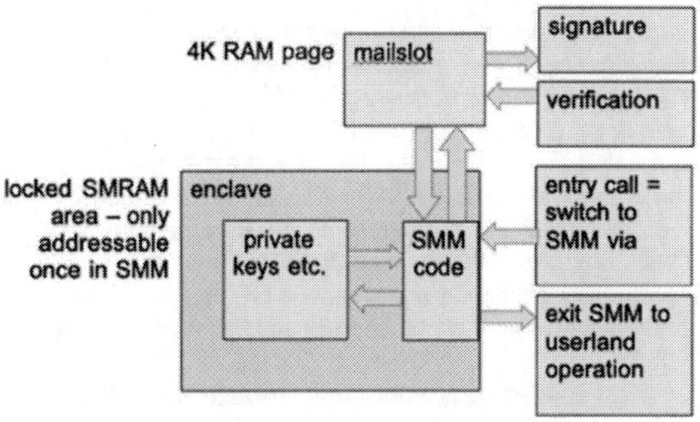

Figure 2. API/Using SMM for signature verification

Userland code inserts any public key to be verified into the mailslot, transitions into SMM (See Section III.A.2 - "Transitioning to SMM" below) which causes a jump to the code in the SMRAM. That code has access to both the mailslot RAM and the SMRAM - verifies the public key against the private key held in SMRAM and places the result of verification(true/false) in the mailslot RAM and exits from SMM causing a return to the calling userland code.

To make use of the cryptographic enclave services, the userspace code must first allocate and lock a page of physical memory, determining the underlying physical address via the Linux /proc/self/pagemap virtual file and communicating this to the SMM enclave at initialisation time. This shared page can then be used as a mailslot for exchanging data: the userspace (ring 3) code interacts directly with the SMM cryptographic code, without transitions to/from the kernel in between.

1) Key negotiation

To protect the most sensitive data requires the construction of some sort of containment to which access from all other components is restricted or prevented — but with just enough interaction permitted to enable the intended use of the keys (or other material) in question. For an SSL/TLS web server, the sensitive data is created as a public/private key pair. As the name implies, the public part of the pair may be freely exported and shared — indeed, it is provided to every client connecting, as part of the initial protocol handshake — while the private key is never to be disclosed to anyone else. To prove the identity of the server, a Certificate Signing Request (CSR) is generated and signed using the private key; after completion of appropriate checks, a Certification Authority (either one trusted by the general public and the software they use, such as LetsEncrypt, or an internal entity such as the US Department of Defense's internal CA) usually signs that CSR to produce a certificate. Any entity can issue certificates, it is merely a matter of policy which issuers are trusted or not for any given situation; for experimental purposes, a self-issued certificate is equally suitable.

2) Transition to SMM

The process of transitioning to SMM is worth examining as it incurs an overhead and as it needs to be accomplished each time a cryptographic verification operation is required, minimising that overhead is a worthwhile goal.

Entry to SMM requires triggering an SMI (System Management Interrupt). Ordinarily, hardware interrupts cannot be triggered directly from user mode applications; first a system call would be required, to effect a transition to kernel mode ('ring 0' on x86), then the corresponding kernel code would trigger the interrupt on the application's behalf. This, however, incurs additional overhead, two mode transitions rather than one. A more efficient approach is for the application to write to the I/O address 0xb2 as explained below.

Most modern processors implement a unified hardware memory map, in which RAM and devices occupy the same address space; x86 has two distinct memory spaces, a 64 kilobyte legacy space accessed via the IN/OUT set of instructions, and a much larger space accessed via standard memory operations.

For devices mapped into the main memory space, the usual memory permissions apply: the appropriate 4 kilobyte (or larger) page could be mapped with appropriate permission bits set. The I/O space has different, fine-grained permissions: the I/O Permissions Bitmap (IOPB) within the Task State Segment (TSS) controls whether access is granted or not to any given byte within the I/O address space. On Linux, the ioperm system call may be used to enable access to any specified I/O address.

To make use of the cryptographic enclave services, the userspace code must first allocate and lock a page of physical memory, determining the underlying physical address via the Linux /proc/self/pagemap virtual file and communicating this to the SMM enclave at initialisation time. This shared page can then be used as a mailslot for exchanging data: the userspace (ring 3) code interacts directly with the SMM cryptographic code, without transitions to/from the kernel in between.

IV. EVALUATION PROCESS

In order to show that the proposed solution is practicable (and establish the hypothesis) three aspects of the proof-of-concept webserver's behaviour were evaluated: functionality, security, and performance. Functionality was demonstrated by testing with a) a number of web-browsers (Experiment 1) and b) an industry-standard test suite (Experiment 2). Security is shown by reasoning from properties of the SMM system. Performance was tested by a) examining the impact on execution time of the overhead of entering and exiting SMM through micro-benchmarking (Experiment 3) and b) comparing the time taken to serve pages i) with no key protection (Experiment 4a) ii) with 'process-separation' based key-protection (Experiment 4b) and iii) with SMM-based key protection (Experiment 4c). A summary is given in Table II below.

TABLE II. LIST OF VALIDATION EXPERIMENTS PERFORMED AND PURPOSE

Num	Experiment	Purpose
1	Use with range of browsers	Verifying basic webserver functionality
2	Qualys - SSL Labs	Verifying webserver SSL protocol compliance
3	Micro-benchmarking	Measuring the 'real-time' overhead imposed by entering and exiting SMM
4a	Comparison of webserver performance with crypto operation performed with 3 different levels of protection	Measuring the rate that pages could be served with crypto-keys handled in-process, i.e., with no protection
4b		Measuring the rate that pages could be served with crypto-keys handled in a separate process, i.e., with process-separation protection
4c		Measuring the rate that pages could be served with crypto-keys handled in SMM

As the webserver's cryptographic code is unmodified – a standard x86/x86-64 implementation of the elliptic curve algorithms – the key performance metric is the additional overhead introduced by transitions to and from SMM. For context, this should be compared with the overhead entailed in a context switch between usermode processes (as applies where the cryptographic code is run in a separate process, as CloudFlare does in their content delivery network's edge devices) and user-kernel mode transitions particularly after implementation of the Kernel Page Table Isolation (KPTI) changes to mitigate the Spectre/Meltdown security issues. Experiments 3 and 4b quantify these.

For a better indication of the real-world performance impact, standard HTTPS benchmarking — downloading static content over encrypted connections in each configuration tested — gives indicative throughput speeds (Experiment 4).

A. *Functionality*

Once the HTTP-over-TLS (HTTPS) server was implemented, a variety of protocol interactions were tested. Initially, standard HTTPS clients (wget, curl, Mozilla Firefox and Google Chrome) were used to verify basic functionality (Experiment 1), and any issues encountered resolved; after this, the more comprehensive industry standard test suite - SSL Labs from Qualys [35] - was employed (Experiment 2).

B. *Security*

The webserver's resistance to RowHammer and Spectre attacks was analysed. While web server performance testing is a well studied and long-established field [36][37], security is more nebulous. In this context, the architecture is intended to provide isolation, and substantial literature has already studied the various possible routes to accessing SMRAM [25] — cache aliasing, Memory-Type Range Registers (MTRR) manipulation; and early BIOS implementations which neglected to enable D_LOCK timeously). It can also be verified empirically that the SMRAM-protected data/code is not exposed, even to the kernel via a scan of the Linux `/dev/mem` device, which can be configured to expose the kernel's view of the entire memory space. Since the SMM protected data has no functioning address except while the processor is executing in SMM, exploits such as Spectre cannot access this data. (Physical level attacks such as RowHammer or address line fault injection could still be effective.)

1) *RowHammer*

The RowHammer attack allows modification of bits in physically adjacent areas of memory, which could theoretically be used to exfiltrate information from the SMM enclave. Integrity checking would provide some protection against this, while ASLR would make such an attack almost impossible — just shifting the code and data by a small random number of bytes each time the system is booted would mean the attacker was operating blindly (able to flip some bits, but without knowledge of which instruction or piece of data is being affected), while the use of 'canary' values around the code and data would make such an attempted attack very unlikely to go undetected. Moreover, given sufficient knowledge of the memory arrangement in use, simply adding a single disused row between the SMM code and data area and memory used by the system would frustrate any RowHammer attempt: it would corrupt only that buffer space, with no effect on the SMM area.

Also, on the specific test hardware used for the majority of this experimentation, the DDR2 memory installed is much less susceptible to RowHammer attacks anyway: exploiting this generally requires DDR3 or newer, due to the smaller feature size and faster access.

A similar approach would also be effective against most direct hardware attacks, such as address line glitching: without knowing the exact address to target, a successful attack would be very much more difficult than against a system without this protection.

2) *Spectre/Meltdown*

The most recent memory protection attacks against vulnerable Intel and ARM processor architectures pose two potential threats against an SMM protection implementation.

Firstly, the Meltdown techniques can be used directly to extract otherwise protected data, for example from kernel buffers, by using the address of that data indirectly then observing side-effects of that operation. This is not applicable to SMM code or data, since there is no address which refers to that memory in the first place. This was empirically verified by Eclypsium[38].

Secondly, the Spectre attacks have been used against system firmware executing in SMM to bypass bounds checks (ibid.) — that issue is avoided entirely in this work by using only fixed size parameters, with no bounds checks or boundaries to be violated.

C. *Performance*

For the performance assessment, two approaches are used: first (Experiment 3), microbenchmarks, measuring the individual components involved in transitions to and from SMM and kernel mode in isolation ; secondly (Experiments 4a - 4c), to measure the overall performance of a web server using different isolation mechanisms, to be able to compare SMM isolation's performance overhead against versions with no isolation of key handling and one which uses process-level isolation which would protect against process level compromise, but not a root or kernel level one as SMM isolation does.

1) *Experiment 3 - Microbenchmarking the mode transition cost*

The experiment described here investigates the performance aspects of using SMM, detailing the performance impact of each transition to and from SMM compared to transitions to kernel space and back which is the dominant factor in the overall performance of the SMM-isolated server.

After prototyping work on the Bochs hardware simulation, a physical target system was required for performance tests. A Lenovo ThinkPad X200 was obtained and loaded with the Libreboot free software project's variant of the open-source Coreboot firmware (Libreboot), including its SMI handler code which could then be freely modified in theory. An unmodified ThinkPad T60, with similar hardware but retaining the original manufacturer's BIOS, served as control, backup and development system, allowing testing of

SMM code under the Qemu-KVM virtualisation system in conjunction with the related SeaBIOS project[39].

The first performance tests focused on comparing the raw latency penalty imposed by the architecture on transitions between userspace and either kernel mode or SMM as appropriate. This would give an early indication of the viability of the overall approach to explore later, as well as determining how much effort might be required to optimise the design for performance to be viable.

Each test consists of executing the function under test multiple times, recording the elapsed time and calculating the time per iteration from that. To ensure consistency, each test was repeated multiple times and checked for outliers. Timing is measured in two ways: the system 'time of day' clock which records times in microseconds and, for the T60 and virtualised system, the processor Time Stamp Counter read via the 'read time-stamp counter' (`RDTSC`) instruction. On recent Intel processors, including those in use here, the time stamp counter advances at a constant rate regardless of power saving modes or clock speed, making this a useful timing measurement. (On earlier implementations, the TSC rate varied with processor speed, making this usage more problematic.)

The operations tested are listed in Table III. Each set of measurements was performed on each test system, to provide a baseline for interpreting performance figures later (see Section V.C). Table IV shows the test platforms used for benchmarking in the experiments.

TABLE III. OPERATIONS TESTED IN MICRO-BENCHMARKING

Operation	Purpose
NOP SMI	Round trip to/from SMM
open-close	System call requiring access to kernel memory
`getpid()`	Trivial system call to reflect minimal kernel transition cost
signing	Execute a cryptographic operation - specifically generate a signed certificate

TABLE IV. TEST PLATFORMS FOR BENCHMARKING

Model	X200	T60	Qemu-VM
CPU	Core 2 Duo P8400	Core 2 Duo T5600	Core 2 Duo T5600
Clockspeed	2.26 GHz	1.83GHz	1.83GHz
RAM	4 GiB	3 GiB	1 GiB
BIOS	Libreboot	Lenovo original	SeaBIOS

The test code was compiled with level 2 optimisation ('-O2'), for x86-64, in each case. To gather statistical details about the distribution of each individual operation, the test code optionally records the TSC value after each; for the overall operations, to avoid the extra overhead, a consecutive sequence of runs is timed without recording timestamps in between, by compiling with the BATCHONLY flag. For the 1,000,000 iterations of `getpid()`, 8,000,000 bytes of values are written out to memory, almost four times the size of the L2 cache, although writing the values to disk is deferred until after the timed portion. Ordinarily the `getpid()` function is accessed via vDSO for performance reasons— the kernel puts a copy of the PID in the process's own memory space and provides a function to retrieve that directly, avoiding the userspace-kernel round trip, but in order to measure that round trip the legacy system call is used here.

The `getpid()` system call was chosen as the most trivial, since it only copies a non-sensitive constant integer; the open system call will be reading the file system cache, which is not readable from user mode, so incurs greater overhead in a full transition to restore access to kernel data. In normal usage `getpid()` is faster than this, avoiding a system call entirely by returning the process's own copy of this value directly via a mechanism known as Virtual Dynamic Shared Object (vDSO).

The 'signing' test measured a realistic cryptographic operation carried out entirely in SMM. For a web server to be accepted as 'valid' for a given name, it must present a signed certificate asserting ownership of that name, signed by either a trusted root Certificate Authority (CA) directly, or an intermediate certificate which is itself trusted.

This is a two stage process. First, a Certificate Signing Request must be generated, containing a copy of the server's public key and a signature using the private key (the private key itself is never exposed). Secondly, this CSR must be submitted to and accepted by the CA. Originally, this was done manually using human verification of documents and credentials; this still applies for 'Extended Validation' certificates, but for standard 'Domain Validation' certificates this process can now be entirely automatic. Specifically, the free "LetsEncrypt" CA allows ownership of a name to be verified by publishing specific challenge response values in the DNS entries of the name in question, without the server ever having to be publicly accessible. This is one variant of the Automated Certificate Management Environment (ACME) protocol; other variants use the TLS SNI handshake process and HTTP messages respectively to accomplish similar results via other protocols.

This allows a public-private keypair to be generated within the SMM enclave, issued with a valid certificate, then used to host a secured website for testing and demonstration purposes, without ever exposing the key material externally. For testing purposes, however, this external signing step is not necessary: a 'self-signed' certificate is sufficient.

2) Experiment 4 - Webserving

The proof-of-concept webserver application was operated (on the local machine to nullify effects of other network traffic) with three different levels of key isolation: none (a control), process separation, and fully SMM isolated key handling. In each case the multiple HTTPS requests for pages of differing sizes where pages were automatically generated (via `curl` etc.) and the rate at which requests were served was measured. This allowed a comparison of the relative speeds of the three levels, which are discussed in Section V.D.

V. RESULTS

The results of the four experiments were thus:

A. Experiment 1 - Basic functionality

Testing with a range of browsers revealed no significant errors.

B. Experiment 2 - Protocol compliance verification

The results of testing with the comprehensive industry standard test suite SSL Labs from Qualys are shown in Figure 3.

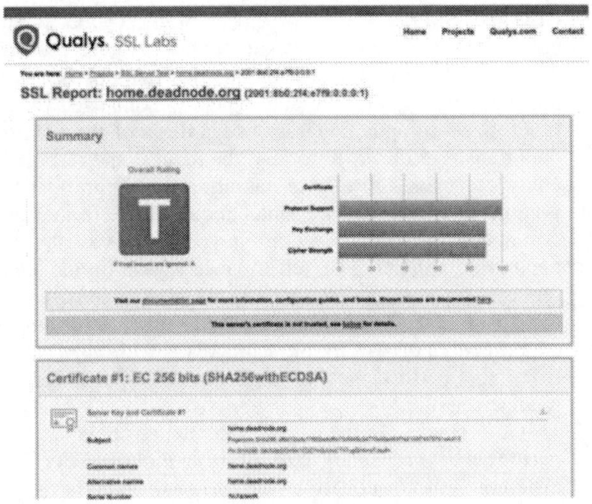

Figure 3. Qualys test suite results

The "T" score indicates a Trust issue — the test server is not configured with a publicly trusted certificate, issued by a genuine Certification Authority such as Verisign or LetsEncrypt — but all cryptographic and protocol aspects are correct; the test suite proceeds to simulate the cryptographic handshakes of a variety of common browsers. With the exception of Google Chrome on Windows XP Service Pack 3, which experiences a handshake failure, all compatible clients negotiate and connect correctly. It is worth noting that no security checks are performed for known vulnerabilities, e.g., Heartbleed etc. – this is purely for compliance with the standard.

C. Experiment 3 - Microbenchmarking the mode transition cost

The timing figures obtained are shown in Tables V, VI and VII below. Unfortunately, the X200 system failed during testing, so further results could not be recorded; the remaining tests had to be performed on the fallback system alone, the T60. SMI calls caused the unmodified T60 control laptop to freeze; this appears to be a known, long-standing issue with the stock Lenovo BIOS[40].

TABLE V. EXECUTION TIME FOR SYSTEM CALLS AND SMI INVOCATIONS

Operation	X200	T60		T60 Qemu-KVM	
Units	µs	µs	TSC	µs	TSC
NOP SMI	448	Not available		1310	2.4m
`getpid`	0.4	1.1	620	21	12k
open/close	3	7.1	3900	26	26k
signing	Not available	878	1.606m	905	1.65m

TABLE VI. EXECUTION TIME (TSC TICKS) ON BARE METAL

Operation	Minimum	1st Quartile	Median	3rd Quartile	Maximum
`getpid`	1133	1155	1155	1155	5211503
open-close	6347	6479	6512	6545	3776872
signing	1534995	1542285.25	1544378	1547757.75	2924856

TABLE VII. EXECUTION TIME (TSC TICKS) UNDER KVM

Operation	Minimum	1st Quartile	Median	3rd Quartile	Maximum
NOP SMI	2235276	2326436.75	2921712.5	3618389	26339800
`getpid`	20229	20295	20317	20361	33031357
open-close	44902	45397	45496	45595	29565196
signing	1536480	1543069	1546578	1596921	12533972

The relative performance of the two hardware test platforms is indicated by comparing the first two columns indicating the T60 has just under half the speed of the X200 on system calls, while comparing the two pairs of T60 figures ('T60' represents the test code running directly under Linux, 'T60 Qemu-VM' represents the same code executed under Qemu-VM simulation) indicates the relative performance penalty of the simulation system itself: approximately three orders of magnitude slowdown (a factor of 1,000). On the most trivial system call, the additional overhead of simulation dominates (as shown by the much smaller difference between getpid and open/close times), but the relative performance of SMI invocation and open/close calls is more similar: 88 times slower in simulation versus 149 times slower on bare metal.

The maximum times for all operations are extreme outliers — around 3-5 million ticks on bare metal, around four times as high under KVM. Each indicates the test application was interrupted during that operation for between 2-20 ms. The additional KVM overhead is most apparent when comparing the getpid operations (a median more than 17 times slower), closing to a factor of 7 for open-close and no discernable difference on cryptographic operations performed in userspace.

The SMI transition overhead is less uniform, with the upper quartile more than 55% higher than the lower — an interesting characteristic, worthy of further study elsewhere.

One important comparison is between the two full mode transitions (userland/SMM and userland/kernel mode). Since the secured server developed here achieves the security benefits by transitioning into SMM before performing each signing operation, the relative performance impact of this change is indicated by the relationship between the 'signing' and 'SMM' figures: the signature operation in isolation takes a little less than the round-trip to and from SMM, 1.6 million processor ticks versus 2.4 million.

D. Experiment 4 - Performance comparison

The rate of request processing, i.e., the number of requests per second served by the webserver, were measured in three configurations (for a range of response sizes 1KiB-MiB) to identify the additional overhead contributed by the use of SMM to isolate the cryptographic private key and associated code. The control configuration (no isolation at all - so no change of mode - labelled Q0) was compared with the simple option (using a separate user-space process for isolation userland to kernel mode transition - Q1) and the SMM configuration (userland - SMM transition- Q2). The measured rates are shown in Figure 4.

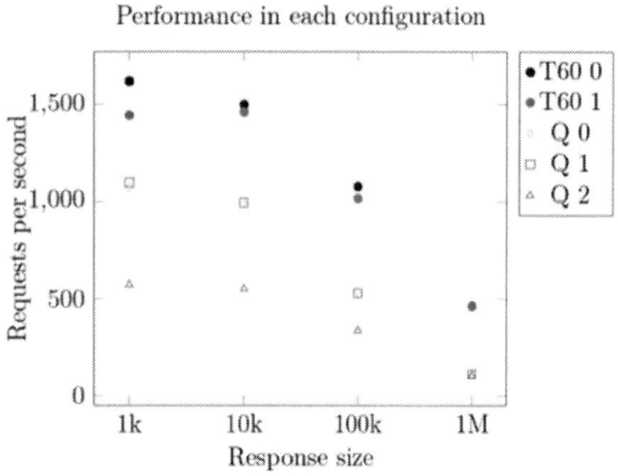

Figure 4. Relative rate of web requests served against response (page) size for each configuration of hardware/enclave type

The performance overhead of simulation as opposed to direct execution is apparent. Across the range of request sizes tested, physical hardware is consistently and proportionally faster than simulated. As the request size increases, the difference between SMM and other modes diminishes to less than 10% at the largest size, one MiB.

VI. Conclusion and Future Work

This work proves the hypothesis: "Secure isolation can be practically implemented using only the long-established Systems Management Mode mechanisms, giving better security isolation than existing techniques such as process separation". In comparison to the baseline approaches (typified by those discussed in Section II) the SMM approach to key-protection has been shown to address their shortcomings and to be robust in circumstances in which they are not. The performance impact of SMM has been explored both on bare hardware and in virtualised form, and a proof-of-concept server demonstrated and benchmarked successfully. Even on relatively old legacy hardware, with additional overhead, the performance impact due to SMM isolation was not prohibitive — approximately doubling the CPU time per handshake operation, causing a performance penalty falling from 50% on the smallest payload sizes (where the handshaking process dominates the overall workload) to 10% at 1 MiB.

A. Implications of results

With a working HTTPS implementation using SMM security, Experiment 4 gave the best indication of SMM's performance impact in the worst case. The relative performance on simulated hardware corroborates the microbenchmark results: performing the cryptographic handshake computations in SMM approximately halves the rate at which handshakes are performed, causing a corresponding slowdown on the smallest requests (where this aspect dominates the overall server performance), falling to around 10% with 1 MiB requests. The effect of size is to be expected: SSL/TLS uses two levels of encryption. First, the connection is established using public key cryptography. This handshake process negotiates two pairs of keys which are then used to encrypt subsequently exchanged data and has a fixed computational cost regardless of the volume of data transferred later. Secondly, the request and response are encrypted using those keys, taking time proportional to the volume involved. So, on small requests the former aspect dominates performance; on larger requests, the latter becomes dominant. The performance shown on the smallest requests, 572 1k requests per second, is also consistent with the bare metal SMM transition measurements from experiment 2 of 448 μs on a processor with approximately twice the performance (a higher clock speed and faster memory bus).

Our results demonstrate the upper bound on the performance or latency cost of isolating the keys in two different ways, validating the original hypothesis about SMM's suitability for this technique. At the smallest extreme of payload sizes, where the cryptographic handshake for each new connection dominates, the additional SMM overhead is of a similar magnitude; as the size increases, the impact of this extra overhead on overall throughput rapidly diminishes.

B. Future work

This work confirms the potential for new uses of SMM in a security context. Unlike reactive patching, SMM isolation provides proactive protection against issues of low-level hardware bugs and protection. Alternative areas for the application of SMM to improve security are discussed below.

1) Intrusion countermeasures

The HyperGuard/HyperCheck projects leveraged SMM as an integrity checking mechanism to detect and alert compromises of a system. These could be incorporated within the application of the SMM: not only would the keys in SMM remain protected, but the compromise would also be detected and appropriate defensive responses could be triggered.

2) Operation batching

When adopting the SMM approach, significant gains in throughput are expected (in a server situation) from performing multiple cryptographic operations per transition to/- from SMM: rather than passing individual requests immediately, combine the requests into sets and process a full set each time. This would amortise the transition cost across however many connection handshakes are being performed in that batch, trading increased throughput for increased latency determined by the batch size.

3) Other applications and protocols

Particularly with the inclusion of other algorithms, the key protection and handling techniques demonstrated here could be applied to other protocols and applications such as SSH authentication, cryptocurrency transactions or a credential store akin to Microsoft's Credential Guard (which uses a special-purpose virtual machine to isolate credentials from the primary OS on desktop systems).

4) Handshaking overhead in TLS 1.3

The latest version of TLS has a faster handshake than TLS 1.2 used in the experiments but the effect of this on the overhead should be verified.

REFERENCES

[1] Y Kim et al., "Flipping bits in memory without accessing them: An experimental study of DRAM disturbance errors". In: ACM SIGARCH Computer Architecture News. Vol. 42 3. IEEE Press, pp. 361–372, 2014

[2] M.Seaborn and T. Dullien, "Exploiting the DRAM rowhammer bug to gain kernel privileges". In: Black Hat, pp. 7–9, 2015

[3] D. Liu et al., "Architectural support for copy and tamper resistant software". In: ACM SIGPLAN Notices 35.11, pp. 168–177, 2000

[4] G. Chen, et al., "SgxPectre Attacks: Leaking Enclave Secrets via Speculative Execution". In: CoRR abs/1802.09085. arXiv: 1802.09085. Url: http://arxiv.org/abs/1802.09085 Retrieved: 2023.06.01.

[5] NVD Spectre – "NVD-CVE-2017-5753 – Spectre", url: https://www.cve.org/CVERecord?id=CVE-2017-5753 Retrieved: 2023.06.0, 2017

[6] J. Sutherland, "On Improving Cybersecurity Through Memory Isolation Using Systems Management Mode", PhD Thesis, Abertay University, Dundee, UK, 2018

[7] F. J. Corbató, M. Merwin-Daggett and R. C. Daley, "An experimental time-sharing system". In: Proceedings of the May 1-3, 1962, spring joint computer conference. ACM, pp. 335–34, 1962

[8] P. J. Denning, "Virtual Memory". In: ACM Comput. Surv. 2.3, pp. 153–189. issn: 0360-0300. doi: 10 . 1145 / 356571 . 356573. url: http://doi.acm.org/10.1145/356571.356573, 1970, Retrieved: 2023.06.01

[9] NVD Heartbleed (2023) - "NVD-CVE-2014-0160 - Heartbleed", url: https://nvd.nist.gov/vuln/detail/CVE-2014-0160 Retrieved: 2023.06.01, 2014

[10] T. Müller, F. C. Freiling and A. Dewald, "TRESOR Runs Encryption Securely Outside RAM." In: USENIX Security Symposium, pp. 17–17, 2011

[11] E-O. Blass and W.Robertson, "TRESOR-HUNT: attacking CPU-bound encryption". In: Proceedings of the 28th Annual Computer Security Applications Conference. ACM, pp. 71–78, 2012

[12] T. Müller, B. Taubmann and F. C. Freiling, "TreVisor". In: Applied Cryptography and Network Security. Springer, pp. 66–83, 2012

[13] T. Shinagawa, et al., "Bitvisor: a thin hypervisor for enforcing i/o device security". In: Proceedings of the 2009 ACM SIGPLAN/SIGOPS international conference on Virtual execution environments. ACM, pp. 121–130, 2009

[14] J. Götzfried and T. Müller, "ARMORED: CPU-bound Encryption for Android-driven ARM Devices". In: Availability, Reliability and Security (ARES), 2013 Eighth International Conference on. IEEE, pp. 161–168, 2013

[15] T. Müller and M. Spreitzenbarth, "Frost". In: Applied Cryptography and Network Security. Springer, pp. 373–388, 2013

[16] B. Spengler, "PaX: The Guaranteed End of Arbitrary Code Execution" (PDF). grsecurity.net. Slides 22 through 35. Retrieved: 2023.06.01, 2003

[17] N. Provos, "Encrypting Virtual Memory." In: USENIX Security Symposium,pp. 35–44, 2000

[18] N. Sullivan, "Keyless SSL: The Nitty Gritty Technical Details", url: https://blog.cloudflare.com/keyless-ssl-the-nitty-gritty-technical-details/ Retrieved: 2023.06.01, 2014

[19] J.Graham-Cumming, "Incident report on memory leak caused by Cloudflare parser bug", url: https://blog.cloudflare.com/incident-report-on-memory-leak-caused-by-cloudflare-parser-bug/ Retrieved: 2023.06.0, 2017

[20] Wikipedia – "Credential Guard" url: https://en.wikipedia.org/wiki/Credential_Guard, Retrieved: 2023.06.0, 2023

[21] S. Bajikar, "Trusted Platform Module (TPM) based Security on Notebook PCs — White Paper". In: Mobile Platforms Group Intel Corporation 1, p. 20., 2002

[22] J. Seo et al., "SGX-Shield: Enabling address space layout randomization for SGX programs", In: Proceedings of the 2017 Annual Network and Distributed System Security Symposium (NDSS), San Diego, CA, 2017

[23] M.Schwarz, S. Weiser, D. Gruss, C. Maurice and S. Mangard, "Malware Guard Extension: Using SGX to Conceal Cache Attacks". In: arXiv preprint arXiv:1702.08719, 2017

[24] P-L. Aublin et al., "TaLoS: Secure and transparent TLS termination inside SGX enclaves". In: Imperial College London, Tech. Rep 5, 2017

[25] R. W. and J. Rutkowska, "Attacking SMM memory via Intel CPU cache poisoning". Online: Invisible Things Lab, url: http://invisiblethingslab.com/resources/misc09/smm_cache_fun.pdf Retrieved: 2023.06.01, 2009

[26] S. Embleton, S. Sparks and C. C. Zou, "SMM rootkit: a new breed of OS independent malware". In: Security and Communication Networks 6.12, pp. 1590–1605, 2013

[27] J. Rutkowska and R. Wojtczuk, "Preventing and detecting Xen hypervisor subversions". In: Blackhat Briefings USA, 2008

[28] J. Wang, A. Stavrou and A. Ghosh, "HyperCheck: A hardware assisted integrity monitor". In: Recent Advances in Intrusion Detection. Springer, pp. 158–177, 2010

[29] B.Ding, Y. He, Y. Wu and Y. Lin, "HyperVerify: a VM-assisted architecture for monitoring hypervisor non-control data". In: Software Security and Reliability-Companion (SERE-C), 2013 IEEE 7th International Conference on. IEEE, pp. 26–34, 2013

[30] K. C. Barde, "Hypervisor security using SMM". US Patent 8,843,742, 2014

[31] A. M. Azab et al., "Hypervision across worlds: Real-time kernel protection from the arm trustzone secure world". In: Proceedings of the 2014 ACM SIGSAC Conference on Computer and Communications Security. ACM, pp. 90–102, 2014

[32] A. van de Ven et al., "Supervisor mode execution protection", US Patent 9,323,533, 2016

[33] OpenSSL, "Simple TLS Server", url: https://wiki.openssl.org/index.php/Simple_TLS_Server, Retrieved 2023.06.01, 2022

[34] Google, "Google's SSL implementation: BoringSSL", url: https://boringssl.googlesource.com/boringssl/ Retrieved: 2023.06.0, 2022

[35] Qualys, "SSL Labs SSL server test", url: https : / / www.ssllabs.com/ Retrieved: 2023.06.0, 2014

[36] G. Trent and M. Sake, "WebSTONE: The first generation in HTTP server benchmarking", 1995

[37] G. Banga and P.Druschel, "Measuring the capacity of a Webserver under realistic loads". In: World Wide Web 2.1-2, pp. 69–83, 1999

[38] Eclypsium, "System Management Mode Speculative Execution Attacks", url: https://eclypsium.com/2018/05/17/system-management-modespeculative-execution-attacks/ Retrieved: 2023.06.01, 2018

[39] SeaBIOS Project, "SeaBIOS", url: https://www.seabios.org/SeaBIOS Retrieved: 2023.06.01.

[40] Ubuntu 2011 - "Lenovo W520 laptop freezes on ACPI-related actions." url: https : / / bugs.launchpad.net/ubuntu/+source/linux/+bug/776999 Retrieved: 2023.06.01

FoodFresh: Multi-Chain Design for an Inter-Institutional Food Supply Chain Network

Philipp Stangl and Christoph P. Neumann
Department of Electrical Engineering, Media and Computer Science
Ostbayerische Technische Hochschule Amberg-Weiden
Amberg, Germany
e-mail: {p.stangl1 | c.neumann}@oth-aw.de

***Abstract*—We consider the problem of supply chain data visibility in a blockchain-enabled supply chain network. Existing methods typically record transactions happening in a supply chain on a single blockchain and are limited in their ability to deal with different levels of data visibility. To address this limitation, we present FoodFresh – a multi-chain consortium where organizations store immutable data on their blockchains. A decentralized hub coordinates the cross-chain exchange of digital assets among the heterogeneous blockchains. Mechanisms for enabling blockchain interoperability help to preserve the benefits of independent sovereign blockchains while allowing for data sharing across blockchain boundaries.**

Keywords-blockchain; consortium; supply chain network; controlled transparency; interoperability.

I. Introduction

The food industry comprises companies dedicated to manufacturing and processing raw materials and semi-finished products from agriculture, forestry, and fishing. In recent years, food supply chains have progressed from shorter, independent to more unified, coherent relationships among supply chain participants [1]. Developing long-term, and collaborative relationships requires evolutionary technological solutions to simultaneously retain a competitive edge.

Blockchain technology is considered a way to increase supply chain visibility, support fraud detection and provide supply chain optimization. Current applications of blockchain technology in food supply chain management, e.g., IBM Food Trust [2], rely mainly on a single distributed ledger. The implications on supply chain networks are twofold: (i) organizations participating in multiple supply chains must share their data on multiple blockchains, and (ii) participants may see information originally not intended for them because all participants can view every transaction on a distributed ledger. In a single-chain approach with just one ledger, all data would be shared publicly will all other chain participants.

The multi-chain requirement is motivated by achieving controlled transparency, i.e., to enable all parties to control visibility of data based on two levels of chains. Each participant is provided with a chain of type *permissioned*, and sharing data is provided by an additional chain of type *public*. The permissioned chains are subject to a Role Based Access Control (RBAC) mechanism, thus, its information is hidden from the public and accessible to all users that belong to an organization. Providing organizations each with their own permissioned chain, interconnecting them as a federated ecosystem with a public chain also simplifies the addition or removal of individual organizations from the overall ecosystem with minimal impact.

In this paper, we propose FoodFresh – a multi-chain approach for inter-institutional supply chain networks, allowing organizations to store immutable data on their blockchain. A decentralized hub coordinates the cross-chain communication among the heterogeneous blockchains. The hub further ensures that all parties comply with the overarching rules of the consortium.

The remainder of the paper is organized as follows: in Section II, a selection of related work is presented. Subsequently, an overview of the relevant technology is given in Section III. Next, Section IV discusses our proposal with the design rationale. We conclude the paper in Section V, followed by the references at the end.

II. Related work

Recently, various solutions for blockchain-enabled supply chains have been proposed. For instance, Longo *et al.* have presented a software connector to connect an Ethereum-like public blockchain with an enterprise information system [3]. The software connector allows companies to share information with their partners with different levels of visibility. Schulz and Freund [4] have proposed a blockchain-enabled distributed supply chain. Their main idea is a network-centric design, which incorporates domain-specific blockchains for handling specific business processes and a hub or main blockchain that connects the blockchains to communicate with each other.

Polkadot uses a hybrid consensus model, separating block production (Blind Assignment of Blockchain Extension (BABE)) from finality (GHOST-based Recursive Ancestor Deriving Prefix Agreement (GRANDPA)). This allows for blocks to be rapidly produced and finalized at a slower pace without risking slower transaction speeds or stalling. Polkadot provides cross-chain communication with arbitrary data. Parachains communicate through the Cross-Chain Message Passing (XCMP) protocol, a queuing communication mechanism based on a Merkle tree. XCMP is designed to communicate arbitrary messages between parachains. Messages are sent together with the next parachain block (short: parablock), while the relay chain blocks include only the proof of postage. All messages must be processed in proper order, for which a chain of Merkle proofs is used. However, XCMP is still under development. Therefore, the stop-gap protocol is Horizontal Relay-routed Message Passing (HRMP). As soon as XCMP is fully developed, it can replace HRMP. The primary difference between the two is the data stored on the relay chain. In HRMP, the relay chain stores the full message with its payload. XCMP, on the other hand, will only store a reference to the payload. The target parachain will be responsible for decoding the message payload.

From the perspective of inter-institutional supply chains, FoodFresh extends our previous work on inter-institutional cooperation [5]–[8] that was focused on healthcare, in which central organizations from primary care and secondary care act as leaders and hubs of cooperation. The FoodFresh scenario extends our perspective to more decentralized and autonomous institutional cooperation in a food supply chain network, without central protagonists.

III. Background

This section provides a brief overview of the different relevant technologies: Section III-A describes the characteristics of food supply chain networks, Section III-B presents different types of blockchain technology, and Section III-C different blockchain interoperability approaches.

A. Food Supply Chain Network

A supply chain is an interconnection of organizations, activities, resources, people, and information. Organizations along a food supply chain are dedicated to growing and processing raw materials (e.g., fruits) and semi-finished products (e.g., fruit juices) for delivery to the end customer. Food supply chains are complex and affected by various factors, such as the sociopolitical environment [9]. Regulatory bodies, such as the US Department of Agriculture (USDA), aim to protect consumer health and increase economic viability. Thus, they release frequent updates to ensure their criteria are met by food supply chains.

In a Food Supply Chain Network (FSCN), more than one supply chain and more than one business process can be identified, both parallel and sequential in time. The parties involved in the business processes depend on the type of FSCN. This article considers a FSCN for fresh agricultural products.

Van der Vorst *et al.* have identified farmers, retailers, and their logistics service suppliers as parties involved in a FSCN for fresh agricultural products [9]. Figure 1 depicts such a supply chain at the organization level within the context of a FSCN for fresh agricultural products. Each organization is positioned in a product lifecycle stage and belongs to at least one supply chain. That means an organization can have multiple suppliers and customers at the same time and over time. Figure 1 visualizes this by showing the perspective of the processor (bold lines), who has multiple connections to distributors and farmers. Other stakeholders, such as nongovernmental organizations, governments, and shareholders, are indirectly involved at each stage of the product lifecycle.

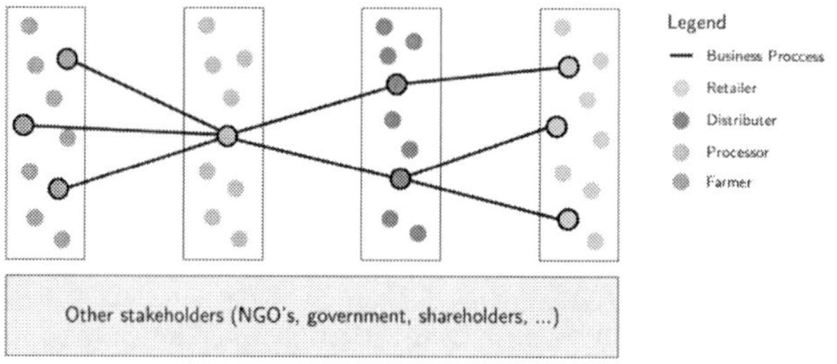

Figure 1. Schematic diagram of an FSCN (based on Van der Vorst *et al.* [9])

B. Blockchain Types

There are three different types of blockchain systems [10]. Public blockchains are considered permissionless because, in principle, everyone can attend the consensus process and read the stored data. The application of public blockchains has several use cases, including cryptocurrencies and document validation. In a consortium blockchain, an elected group of participants is allowed to attend the consensus process. The stored data may be read by selected members or by the public. Supply chain and research environments are two exemplary use cases for this type of blockchain. In a private blockchain, all participants belong to the same organization, and the public cannot access the system. Two use cases for this final blockchain type are banking and asset ownership. Private and consortium blockchains are considered permissioned blockchains because, in both cases, only a limited group can attend the consensus process.

C. Blockchain Interoperability

Blockchain interoperability involves the ability of independent distributed ledger networks to communicate with each other. Various approaches have been established to provide blockchain interoperability, resulting in a highly fragmented market [11]. Belchior *et al.* were the first to conduct a systematic literature review in [11] on blockchain interoperability solutions: Their resulting Blockchain Interoperability Framework categorizes interoperability solutions into three categories: 1) interoperability across public blockchains (public connectors), 2) independent blockchains that interoperate among each other (blockchains of blockchains), and finally, 3) approaches that neither fit into the public connectors nor blockchains of blockchains category (hybrid connector).

IV. FoodFresh

In this section, we describe a consortium blockchain for a food supply chain network for interoperability and controlled transparency. Section IV-A, introduces the approach. The three tiers of the system architecture are described in the following sections: the presentation tier in Section IV-B1, the application tier in Section IV-B2, and the relay tier in Section IV-B3. In Section IV-C, we offer a concise introduction to the Substrate Framework. The subsequent Section IV-D, delineates the details concerning the deployment process. Finally, Section IV-E addresses the limitations of our proposed approach.

A. FoodFresh Approach

The FoodFresh approach provides an implementation of the multi-chain approach (Section II). The blockchain consortium comprises a multi-chain ecosystem for organizations. Each organization is allowed to participate in the consensus process. A permanent and shared record of food system data connects participants across the food supply chain network. This is done through the use of a main blockchain, called relay chain. The sole purpose of the relay chain is to coordinate and share appropriate data and ensure all parties are complying with overarching rules. Each organization can set up and manage its own permissioned blockchain, which keeps full control over the data to itself. Within a single permissioned blockchain for an organization, data is shared between different users that belong to that organization, but not to inter-institutional parties. Via the public relay, the FoodFresh approach allows them to share immutable and accurate data with other participants in the inter-institutional supply network. This also allows for the addition or removal of individual organizations from the overall ecosystem with minimal impact.

B. System Architecture

FoodFresh, as a distributed system, is a composition of three tiers. This section will outline each of the three tiers. The presentation tier in Section IV-B1, the application tier in Section IV-B2, and finally the relay tier in Section IV-B3. Figure 3 depicts the system architecture for two interoperating supply chain organizations.

1) Presentation Tier: To provide the user with convenient access to the FoodFresh system, the presentation tier is responsible for interacting with the application tier through a websocket connection. Any websocket-capable client or device can communicate with the endpoints exposed by the application tier. The user interacts with a Graphical User Interface (GUI) to manage the permissions of participating members, register shipments and products, and trace shipments along the supply chain. A browser extension is required to manage blockchain accounts and to sign transactions within those accounts.

2) Application Tier: The application tier encompasses application-specific blockchains (the parachains) that allow organizations to join with their blockchain, where they can store immutable data. Through this, organizations can create products and shipments. A shipment's storage and transportation conditions can be monitored and tracked through the supply chain. The business logic is decomposed in tightly coupled modules called pallets. Figure 2 depicts the business logic pallets, each with its provided functionality that can be invoked via transactions on the parachain. Additionally, an Off-Chain Worker (OCW) is used to communicate the latest shipment status with the external world. With the subsystem Cumulus, parachains can send and receive cross-chain messages and enable validators to validate their state transitions. RBAC, formalized by Ferraiolo *et al.* [12], has become the predominant model for user access control. RBAC is used in the FoodFresh approach to control the access in terms of who can submit transactions. The *rbac* pallet maintains an on-chain registry of roles and the users to which those roles are assigned. A role is a tuple with the name of a pallet and a permission that qualifies the level of access granted by the role. A permission is an enumeration with the variants *Execute* and *Manage*. The *Execute* permission allows a user to invoke a pallet's dispatchable functions. The *Manage* permission allows a user to assign and revoke roles for a pallet, and also implies the *Execute* permission. Access control validation is done within the transaction pool of a parachain.

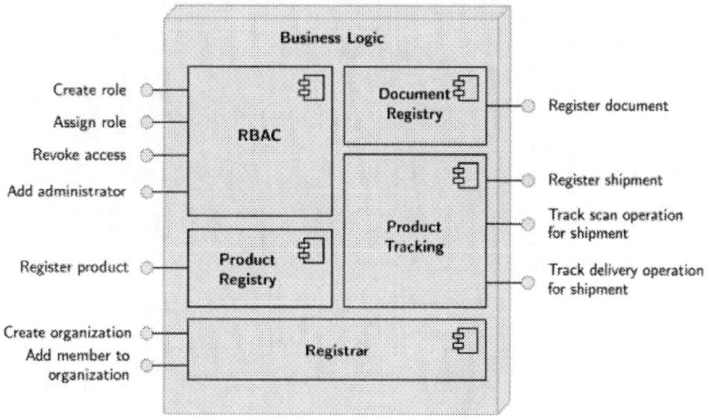

Figure 2. Overview of the business logic, decomposed into five pallets

3) Relay Tier: The relay chain, in the relay tier, is the essential hub in the network of heterogeneous blockchains, the parachains. The relay chain provides parachains with parablock validation and allows them to communicate with each other using the Cross-Chain Messaging (XCM) format for cross-chain messaging.

Validators are the actors of the relay chain and have three responsibilities: (1) to verify that the information contained in parablocks is valid, such as the identities of the transacting parties, (2) to participate in the consensus mechanism to produce the relay chain blocks based on validity statements from other validators, and (3) to handle cross-chain messages. For validators to fulfill their responsibilities, they are equipped with six primary runtime modules. The *inclusion* module handles the inclusion and availability of parablocks. In addition, *shared* manages the shared storage and configurations for other validator

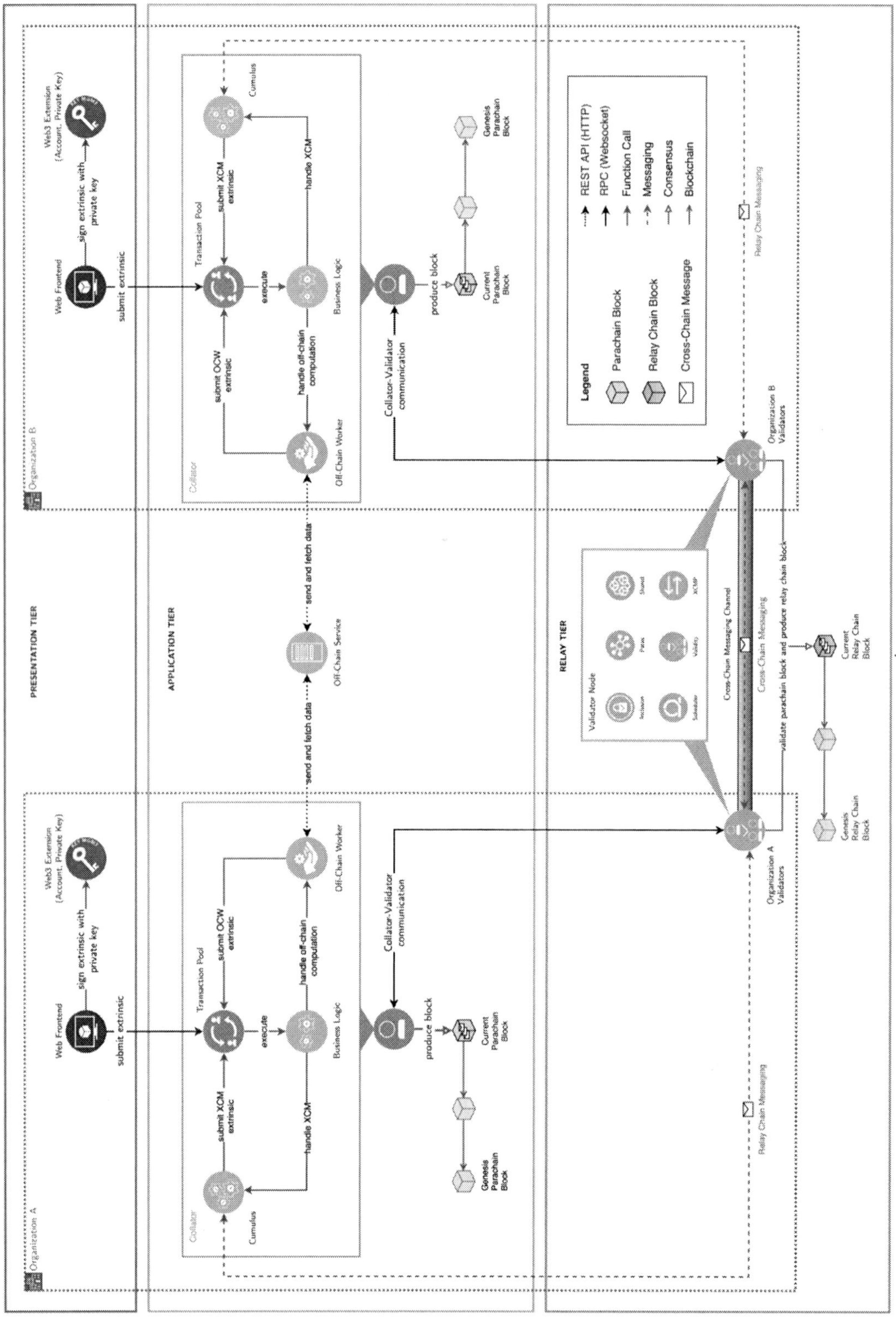

Figure 3. Overview of our approach. The architecture is composed of three tiers: presentation, application, and relay.

modules. The *paras* module manages the chain-head and validation code for parachains. The *scheduler* is responsible for parachain scheduling, as well as validator assignments for the consensus mechanism. The *validity* module addresses secondary checks and disputes resolution for available parablocks. Finally, the *XCMP* module handles cross-chain messages and ensures that the messages are relayed to the receiving parachain.

An integral part of cross-chain communication is the establishment of a cross-chain messaging channel between the validators of two communicating parachains. Burdges *et al.* [13] have stated that a messaging channel aims to guarantee four things: "First that messages arrive quickly; second that messages from one parachain arrive to another in order; third that arriving messages were indeed sent in the finalized history of the sending chain; and fourth that recipients will receive messages fairly across senders, helping guarantee that senders never wait indefinitely for their messages to be seen".

The act of removing an organization from the ecosystem does not necessitate the elimination of its associated parachain. This concept is facilitated by the existence of a systematic protocol, specifically the modification of the relay chain validator registry. Through the processes of registration and deregistration, organizations are added to and removed from this registry. Structurally, this registry is characterized as a hash map, a data structure that comprises paired elements: a unique identifier (ID) and the corresponding parachain ID. It should be noted that the relationship between organizations and their parachains is fundamentally non-destructive, meaning that the alterations in the organization's status within the ecosystem do not directly impinge on the existence of the related parachain.

C. Substrate Framework

FoodFresh is built with substrate [14], a modular framework for building blockchains. A nontechnical reason for using substrate is its flexibility. Organizations must be able to adapt their blockchain system to meet the supply chain compliance requirements of regulatory bodies. Regulations happen frequently, especially in food supply chains, as shown in Section III-A. Due to the modular nature of substrate-based blockchains, developers have the necessary freedom to swap or add modules to their blockchain runtime.

Technical reasons include the chosen programming language, the software design, and the off-chain abilities. Substrate is implemented in the programming language Rust, which aims to provide performance (comparable to C++), reliability, and better means of productivity. In terms of reliability, Rust manages resources (including memory, files, network, and thread) and avoids problems, such as resource leaks or data races. Finally, for productivity, Rust provides Integrated Development Environment (IDE) support and type inspections. Furthermore, substrate is generic by design, meaning transactions are abstracted to so-called extrinsics (things that happen outside the chain) and intrinsics (things that happen inside the chain). Transactions are stored as binary large objects. As a result, users can transfer and store any type of data on the blockchain.

Nonetheless, with FoodFresh as a permissioned blockchain, concerns about off-chain processes need to be raised. For instance, Helliar *et al.* have made the assumption that "off-chain processes may become a major barrier for permissioned blockchains" [15]. Using substrate, off-chain data can be queried or processed before it is included in the on-chain state through OCW, a collator node subsystem that allows for the execution of long-running and possibly nondeterministic tasks. Moreover, an OCW does not influence the block production time.

D. Deployment

FoodFresh requires validator nodes for the relay chain and collator nodes for the parachains to be set up by the organizations participating in a supply chain network. Nodes can be deployed locally or remotely via a cloud service provider, such as Amazon Web Services. Before parachains can participate in cross-chain communication, they need to be registered on the relay chain. The following rule is defined in the Collator Protocol [16], which implements the network protocol for the Collator-to-Validator networking: To accept n parachain connections, $n+1$ validator nodes need to run on the relay chain. For the FoodFresh prototype, two relay chain nodes are started to connect one parachain node. Further, the relay chain needs to obtain the hex-encoded parachain's genesis state (exported from a collator node) and the WebAssembly runtime validation function to validate parablocks.

E. Limitations

While the FoodFresh approach offers a comprehensive framework for leveraging blockchain technology in food supply chain management, there are several potential limitations and areas of concern, including:

Scalability: Parachains might face scalability challenges, depending on the scale of the organizations involved and the number of transactions. These issues are typically dependent on their specific implementation, the consensus mechanism used, and the volume of transactions they handle. If an organization's parachain is not optimized to handle large quantities of data or high transaction throughput, it could become a bottleneck that slows down the overall system's performance.

Complexity of Implementation: The FoodFresh approach, with each organization having its own blockchain and one relay chain for cross-communication, increases the complexity of the system compared to commonly used single blockchains. This presents significant challenges in terms of maintenance and understanding the system for non-technical stakeholders.

Adoption Challenges: Organizations might be reluctant to adopt the proposed approach due to perceived risks, lack of understanding, or the costs involved in implementation and training.

Evaluation: The software prototype is implemented and available on GitHub [17] under Apache License 2.0. A key part of designing a supply-chain network is ensuring the network is versatile enough to cope with future risks. The current solutions to analyze and mitigate endogenous risks lack continuous monitoring, as a result, risks from irregularities (e.g. abnormal order quantities by retailers) remain mostly undetected. Thus, a core part of our future evaluation is to answer whether we can develop an approach to detect abnormal activity in a multi-chain scenario. Our plans will focus on capturing the variability of transfer volume in cross-chain messaging in order to detect abnormal activity in blockchain-enabled inter-institutional supply chain networks.

V. Conclusion and Future Work

Developing long-term and increasingly collaborative relationships among supply chain participants requires advanced technological solutions to retain a competitive edge. Blockchain is presented as a promising technology that might increase supply chain visibility and improve efficiency. We have presented FoodFresh – a multi-chain consortium for an inter-institutional food supply chain network. This approach overcomes the challenges associated with current approaches (e.g., IBM Food Trust), such as lack of controlled transparency and restricted interoperability among supply chain participants. By implementing a multi-chain consortium with an overseeing decentralized hub, FoodFresh allows organizations to maintain their independent blockchains, thereby preserving data sovereignty and enabling effective data exchange across blockchain boundaries. The design approach used for FoodFresh could apply to other networks that require the distribution or transfer of sensitive data. Future work could apply the approach to other industries, for instance, healthcare. The safe and secure transfer of patient health records or other sensitive information between healthcare providers, insurance companies, and the patients themselves is a major concern in the healthcare industry. The presented approach could allow each party to maintain control over their data while enabling necessary data sharing.

References

[1] M. A. Bourlakis and P. W. H. Weightman, *Food supply chain management*. John Wiley & Sons, 2008.

[2] IBM Corporation, "About IBM food trust," Jun. 2019, [Online]. Available: https://www.ibm.com/downloads/cas/8QABQBDR (visited on 05/23/2023).

[3] F. Longo, L. Nicoletti, A. Padovano, G. d'Atri, and M. Forte, "Blockchain-enabled supply chain: An experimental study," *Computers & Industrial Engineering*, vol. 136, pp. 57–69, 2019.

[4] K. F. Schulz and D. Freund, "A Multichain Architecture for Distributed Supply Chain Design in Industry 4.0," in *International Conference on Business Information Systems*, Springer, 2018, pp. 277–288.

[5] C. P. Neumann, *Distributed Case Handling*. München: Verlag Dr. Hut, 2013, ISBN: 9783843909198.

[6] C. P. Neumann, F. Rampp, M. Daum, and R. Lenz, "A Mediated Publish-Subscribe System for Inter-Institutional Process Support in Healthcare," in *Proc of the 3rd ACM Int'l Conf on Distributed Event-Based Systems (DEBS 2009)*, Nashville, TN, USA, Jul. 2009, 14:1–14:4.

[7] C. P. Neumann and R. Lenz, "The alpha-Flow Approach to Inter-Institutional Process Support in Healthcare," *International Journal of Knowledge-Based Organizations (IJKBO)*, vol. 2, no. 4, pp. 52–68, 2012.

[8] C. P. Neumann and R. Lenz, "A Light-Weight System Extension Supporting Document-based Processes in Healthcare," in *Proc of the 3rd Int'l Workshop on Process-oriented Information Systems in Healthcare (ProHealth'09) in conjunction with the 7th Int'l Conf on Business Process Management (BPM'09)*, Ulm, DE, Sep. 2009, pp. 557–568.

[9] J. Van der Vorst, A. Beulens, and T. van Beek, "Innovations in logistics and ICT in food supply chain networks," *Innovation in Agri-Food systems*, pp. 245–291, Jan. 2005.

[10] Z. Zheng, S. Xie, H. Dai, X. Chen, and H. Wang, "An overview of blockchain technology: Architecture, consensus, and future trends," in *2017 IEEE International Congress on Big Data*, IEEE, 2017, pp. 557–564.

[11] R. Belchior, A. Vasconcelos, S. Guerreiro, and M. Correia, "A Survey on Blockchain Interoperability: Past, Present, and Future Trends," *ACM Computing Surveys (CSUR)*, vol. 54, no. 8, pp. 1–41, 2021.

[12] D. Ferraiolo, D. R. Kuhn, and R. Chandramouli, *Role-based access control*. Artech house, 2003.

[13] J. Burdges *et al.*, "Overview of polkadot and its design considerations," *ArXiv*, vol. abs/2005.13456, 2020.

[14] Parity Technologies, "Substrate - The Blockchain Framework for a Multichain Future," 2020, [Online]. Available: https://substrate.io/ (visited on 05/23/2023).

[15] C. V. Helliar, L. Crawford, L. Rocca, C. Teodori, and M. Veneziani, "Permissionless and permissioned blockchain diffusion," *International Journal of Information Management*, vol. 54, pp. 102–136, 2020, ISSN: 0268-4012.

[16] Parity Technologies, "Collator Protocol," Jun. 2021, [Online]. Available: https://paritytech.github.io/polkadot/book/node/collators/collator-protocol.html (visited on 05/23/2023).

[17] P. Stangl and C. P. Neumann, "FoodFresh," May 2023, [Online]. Available: https://github.com/cyberlytics/FoodFresh (visited on 05/23/2023).

A Survey of Multiple Clouds: Classification, Relationships and Privacy Concerns

Reem Al-Saidi
School of Computer Science
University Of windsor
Windsor, Canada
Email:alsaidir@uwindsor.ca

Ziad Kobti
School of Computer Science
University Of windsor
Windsor, Canada
Email:kobti@uwindsor.ca

***Abstract*—When major Cloud Service Providers (CSPs) network with other CSPs, they show a predominant area over cloud computing architecture, each with different roles to serve user demands better. This creates multiple clouds computing environments, which overcome the limitations of cloud computing and bring a wide range of benefits (e.g., avoiding vendor lock-in problem). Numerous applications can use various multiple clouds types depending on their specifications and needs. Deploying multiple clouds under hybrid or public models has introduced various privacy concerns that affect users and their data in a specific application domain. To understand the nuances of these concerns, the present study conducted a survey to identify the various classifications of multiple clouds types and then extend the cloud entities' relationships to behave in different multiple clouds settings. The survey results outline users' privacy and data confidentiality concerns in multiple clouds types under public and hybrid deployment models.**

Keywords-multi-cloud; federated cloud; cross-federated cloud; hybrid federated cloud; inter-cloud; cloud interoperability; privacy; trust.

I. INTRODUCTION

Utilizing numerous clouds has emerged as an alternative way to improve cloud computing capacity for massive and real-time data [1] [2]. Collaboration and communication between clouds, known as "Cloud Interoperability" will improve data reliability and resource availability, resulting in high-quality services [3]. Moreover, allowing clouds to connect brings further benefits to the cloud users by avoiding vendor lock-in and getting access to widely distributed resources across different clouds with good performance and legislation-compliant services to the users [3]–[6]. Different applications which produce huge amounts of data realize the importance of multiple clouds to outsource their data and services for better processing and analysis. For example, in the Internet of Things (IoT) applications outsourcing the data to different clouds for further processing overcomes the devices' limited storage and processing capacities [2]. The devices are connected to the internet clouds to accommodate the massive amount of the produced data by each device; processing the data at the edge provides low latency, efficient computation capabilities, and storage capacities [2]. Despite multi-cloud's resource availability, data reliability and scalability [3]–[6], maintaining cloud interoperability while preserving users' privacy and data security is still a significant challenge [3]. Without the users' consent, their data can be stored in another CSPs with different access rules and data processing requirements [7]–[10]. Furthermore, it becomes difficult to guarantee that data is effectively protected through its entire life-cycle, including data creation, storage, processing, transfer, and deletion; different CSPs may have different security policies, methods, and procedures for data processing and storage [7]. It is also more challenging to guarantee the consistency of security policies across all CSPs during data transfer and access, and protect the data against potential threats [16]–[18]. Moreover, identifying the access roles and sharing privileges among different CSPs while maintaining user-sensitive attribute without performance degradation is another critical concern while deploying multiple clouds [22].

Different application domains benefit from multiple clouds deployments [2] [19] [20] [22]. In the health era, various health institutions can share their data and collaborate with other researchers and healthcare professionals, enabling real-time collaboration and improving personal health and treatments [22].

While multi-cloud facilitates seamless data exchange and sharing across different health institutions, it also raises privacy and security concerns concerning data access and sharing processes [58]–[61] [63], [64]. Unauthorized and unrestricted access could expose patient information, compromising privacy and confidentiality. Moreover, the unrestricted data sharing beyond the intended purpose increases privacy risks and the potential for data misuse. Considering the privacy and security issues across various cloud deployment models through different applications reduces the data disclosure risks and highlight the possibilities of applications vulnerabilities.

Without question, user privacy and data security are of the highest importance in the digital age and have attracted much more attention with the adoption of multiple clouds computing. The success of such adoption towards building trustworthy multiple clouds environments is primarily driven by cloud user privacy and data security [9] [10].

There is no generalization for specific security and privacy-preserving approaches in the multiple clouds. It is mainly based on a specific context and the entities involved under a specific multiple clouds type.

The main contributions of this survey are the following:

- Show the classification of multiple clouds types from the state-of-the-art work.
- Investigate the challenges for public and hybrid deployment models in multiple clouds types.
- Extend the single cloud entity's relationships to behave in different types of multiple clouds environment.
- Identify the privacy concerns in the multi-cloud, federated, cross-federated, and inter-cloud under public and hybrid deployment models at some application domains.

The rest of this survey is organized as follows: In Section II, we introduce different types of multiple clouds and their corresponding classification. In Section III, we highlight different difficulties and challenges associated with the various multiple clouds deployment models. In Section IV, we extend the cloud entities relationships to behave under different kinds of multiple clouds. In Section V, we explain the privacy issues in different multiple clouds types under hybrid deployment model. Where appropriate, we reflect these privacy concerns on some applications. Moreover, we highlight the main challenges of different cloud types under specific deployment models. In the end, in Section VI, we summarize the survey work and show the future directions.

II. MULTIPLE CLOUDS CLASSIFICATION

Multiple clouds mean the connection of more than one cloud. It is similar somehow to the set of an inter-connected cloud of clouds. In [4], they introduced the inter-connected global clouds of clouds, it is called the "Inter-Cloud", in which clouds interact and share the resources and the underlying infrastructure to meet the user's on-demand requests. Inter-cloud dynamically allows the management of resources and distributes the loads among different clouds for better resource utilization and service performance. Most researchers consider multiple clouds the same as inter-cloud [1] [11] [12]. Both are classified into multi-cloud and federated cloud based on how clients interact with the clouds.

Inter-cloud is defined as a "maximal set of inter-connected clouds so that no other organization exists outside the inter-cloud domain" [12]. However, some researchers consider inter-cloud as a federated cloud [13] while others [12] claim that the federated cloud is a type of inter-cloud. In [13], they stated the main differences between federated and inter-cloud; the federated cloud is a pre-requisite to the inter-cloud. In a federated cloud, all federated members would have a common perceptive of the applications deployment process [29] [30] while the inter-cloud is based on standards and open interfaces [13]. Federated cloud promises to deploy in different fields, including the academic domain, by building the community cloud with grid computing [19] [20] [28]. Others [16] consider federated cloud as a multi-cloud with a hybrid deployment model.

Inter-cloud is classified into multi and federated clouds [11] [12]. Multi-cloud defines in [15] as "an evolution of cloud computing where different services like Software as a Service (SaaS), Platform as a Service (PaaS), and Infrastructure as a Service (IaaS) are provided based on the organization demands from various cloud service providers".

Multi-cloud enterprises can get services from more than one CSP. It highlights two subcategories: the hybrid and rain cloud [16]. In a rain cloud, each cloud member completes a Service Level Agreement (SLA) with other members enabling different members to work together when data get too large for any of them to handle [17]. SLA works only in a single or private organization, and it is not reliable under public cloud systems [17] [45]. Based on the resources and service provisioning by the broker, multi-cloud is classified into two implementation categories: services and libraries [18]. The federation term refers to the organizational structure where multiple enterprises have set up collaborative agreements known as "Federated Level Agreements (FLA)" [19].

The federation facilitates the adoption of cloud computing within different companies; the private cloud is built internally within the enterprises' scope and connected when necessary to the public cloud for on-demand resource leasing [14] [19] [20]. The federation should be capable of allowing location-free virtual applications deployment across federated sites. These applications can migrate from one site to another partially or completely [19]–[21]. The objective of the federation is to allow collaboration and resource sharing among different cloud providers. It is more appropriate to deploy the federated cloud when a few businesses are willing to cooperate and share their resources to serve the cloud user better [19]–[21].

Signing FLA is simpler when there are a few organizations, it gets challenging when there are several. The user access to the CSP is transparent; which means that users benefit from the federated cloud without being aware of which cloud provider supports the service [21]–[23]. Federation construction among different service providers has many benefits (e.g., increasing the economy of scale, efficient use of the resources and assets, and expansion of providers capabilities) [23]. Maintaining security, privacy, and independence between the federation members is necessary for trustworthy cloud federation construction. There are two types of federated cloud: horizontal federation and cross-cloud federation [1] [24].

The horizontal federation takes place on one level of the cloud stack, e.g., the application stack. Customers may profit from lower costs and better performance, while providers may offer more sophisticated services [1] [23]–[26]. The disadvantage of the horizontal federation is the lack of services scalability and diversity, it can not dynamically meet the changing customers' needs in the application.

Most CSPs that offer comparable services are horizontally federated; the members of the federation offer slightly different services. Thus, limiting the ability of the federated members to scale once user demands for new services increase. Furthermore, while CSPs compete with one another to increase their benefits and reputation, they are reluctant to pool resources or work together in specific contexts, thus limiting the diversity of services offered [23]–[26].

From the developer's point of view, the infrastructure management of federated cloud is easy to develop and maintain through the different federation members via a standard Application Programming Interface (API) [11].

The federation achieves a traffic load balancing among the members to accommodate unusual spikes in resource demands [23] [24]. Moreover, building a federation is less costly than each organization expanding its infrastructure [1] [23] [24]. Implementing a federated cloud overcomes the vendor lock-in problem associated with a single cloud and provider integration concerns [24]. However, federation still suffers from the contention problem where in [27]–[30] addressed the issue and suggested a solution accordingly.

There are many challenges with the federation construction (e.g., performance and disaster recovery through co-location and geographic distribution, expressing the FLA requires translating the abstract requirements to understandable properties for effective organization implementation, and supporting the vertical expansion of the service layer [24]).

In the cross-cloud federation [6], two or more unfamiliar CSPs agree to collaborate during run time. It provides dynamic and diverse benefits to CSPs for expanding their service at run time to better serve the users changing demands. Still, the main challenge in the cross-cloud federation is building the chain of trust from the cloud user to the home cloud, followed by a series of foreign cloud-transitive trust [1]. Another challenge is finding a standardized interface for resource access among cloud domains each with different architectures, policies, and implementations [6].

In [1], they show the several phases of the cross-cloud federation, starting from the discovery of another CSP, called "Foreign Cloud," that wishes to share its federated resources. The home CSP triggers the need for resource leasing as it can not serve the user's requests. The foreign CSP has the minimum user specifications, it will lease its additional federated resource, and be part of the federation construction. The foreign CSP can either have the same requested service forming the intralayer or can pass the request through its stack and delegate the process to the middleware to install the required service forming the interlayer [26].

A Cross-Cloud Federation Manager (CCFM) is the trusted party that makes the negotiations with the foreign cloud, starting from the discovery and resource matching ending with the resource access. CCFM bridges the gap between different service providers through various stages [1] [6].

In conclusion, several perspectives exist on classifying multiple clouds; some consider federated clouds as inter-cloud [13]. Others disagree and claim that federated cloud is a type of inter-cloud [12]. The following classification outlines our categorization of multiple clouds; the inter-cloud is the main category of multiple clouds, classified into multi-cloud and federated clouds. The federated cloud has two main subtypes: horizontal federation and cross-cloud federation.

From our perspective, Figure 1 summarizes the classification of different cloud types.

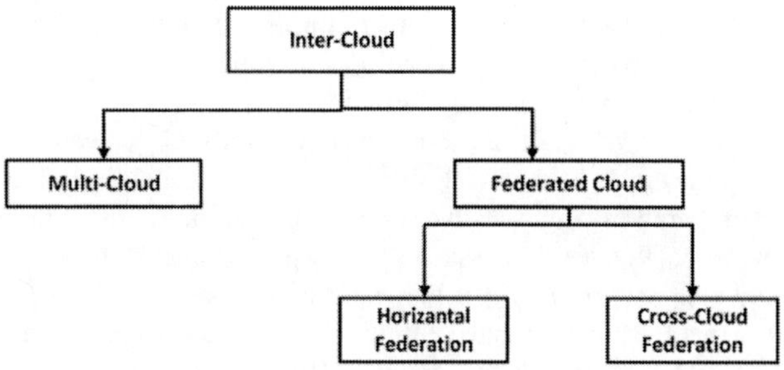

Figure 1: Multiple clouds classification.

III. Difficulties with multiple clouds deployment models

Multiple clouds consist of different elements that can be varied based on specific cloud types and application domains [30]. Moreover, there are different deployment models, including private cloud, public cloud, hybrid cloud, and community cloud [31]. Each deployment model implemented among different types of multiple clouds introduces a wide variety of challenges [32].

Private cloud [21] [31] [32] is a specific computing infrastructure owned and controlled by an organization (enterprise) to serve a group of users in a specific application domain. It can be classified in two main categories:

- Cloud portfolio, in which more than private cloud belongs to the same organization share the same private cloud infrastructure. They didn't compete with each other as they belong to the same organization domain. They can easily initiate cooperation requests with each other and increase the organization revenues [12].
- Independent, a separate cloud each with its own infrastructure and resources and not forming a part of cloud portfolio [21] [32] .

Generally, the private cloud has several challenges and issues including vendor lock-in, trust, security and privacy, cost, scalability and availability [21] [32]. Public cloud [33]–[35] in which prominent vendors and well-known service providers support a wide range of competing services in the marketplace. The services are available to a wide range of interested users upon subscription. The public cloud deployment model supports a multi-tenant feature of cloud computing where different users can share the same pool of storage infrastructure [33]–[36] [46].

Still, deploying the public cloud faces different challenges and concerns [31] [32] [34]–[36], mainly the trust issue becomes the most evident one under the uncertainty and loss of control in the multiple clouds environment. Building trust in the public cloud towards their users will assure them about their data confidentiality and cloud provider commitment and ethical behavior. Implementing a secure infrastructure while keeping the privacy of user attribute and data with a high level of assurance is the first step towards building a trustworthy multiple clouds environment. However, the communication between private and public clouds forms a hybrid deployment model known as "Cloud bursting" in which a private cloud can extend its resource by initiating a request to an external provider as it can't serve its user demands [37]. Even deploying the hybrid model shows promise of enabling cloud interoperability and scalable services provisioning, it still faces many challenges and issues [37]–[40]. The main challenges and concerns in hybrid deployment model are:

1. Trust [38] [39] : trusted entities like a broker or middleware facilitate communication among cloud entities and monitor resource provisioning and access processes between private and public clouds. Cloud users should trust the public cloud provider as they will lose control over their outsource data and services running over the public cloud. A high degree of trust is required so that more users can join a public provider and benefit from its services and applications.
2. Security and privacy [40]: different security regulations and privacy compliance control user data and cloud provider behavior. Due to the lack of user control and the high level of users' uncertainty about the public cloud's commitment. Different privacy and security techniques should be implemented during all data life cycles highlighting different contexts and scenarios.

On the community cloud deployment, resources are owned and controlled by different cloud providers in the community [41]. It has a security and privacy concerns as same as the other deployment models [41].

IV. Entities' relationships on multiple clouds

NIST [42] defined the cloud's five main components: cloud users/consumers, providers, carriers, auditors, and brokers. Each of these entities has different tasks based on a specified setting. We will consider the same entities in the context of multiple clouds and extend their interactions and relationships to behave in a distributed manner. Multiple clouds consist mainly of cloud user(s), cloud provider(s), cloud auditor(s), cloud trusted party as broker(s) or identity providers (IdPs), and cloud carrier(s).

The entities have a context relationship determined by user activities and the type of multiple clouds in use. They have the same definition provided by NIST [42] with some extensions to accommodate the distributed nature of multiple clouds. The elements form the multiple clouds, and their definitions [42] are listed below:

1) Cloud user/consumer(s) are an enterprise, or individuals with internet access looking for better services to meet their demands.
2) Cloud providers/ data center(s) are vendors that offer different types of services (platform, infrastructure, storage, software, artificial intelligence functionalities) on different domains. It supports cloud users with different service and resource leasing based on a pre-defined signed agreements.
3) Cloud-trusted entities facilitate a reliable service delivery between users and providers or among providers themselves. The trusted entities vary based on the type of cloud, e.g., brokers used in the federated, inter-cloud, and cross-cloud federation with an intermediate role. The trusted entities can assist the customer in selecting the most suitable service, manage the dimensionality, heterogeneity, and user uncertainties towards their data and the CSPs [43].

   Brokers in inter or meta cloud can handle the discovery of suitable resources and subsequent data life cycle management [11]. In the context of a cross-cloud federation, the trusted party CCFM is used in the discovery, resource matching, and authentication between home and foreign clouds when the first is saturated in its resources [25]. IdPs act as trusted entities in the cross-cloud federation to establish trust and secure communication between home and foreign clouds for resource access and sharing [1] [25].
4) Cloud auditor(s) perform an assessment of services, performance and security to comply to the regulations and the pre-defined agreements between different entities in the cloud.
5) Cloud carrier(s) support the connectivity and transformation of the cloud services in the underlying network infrastructure across different clouds.

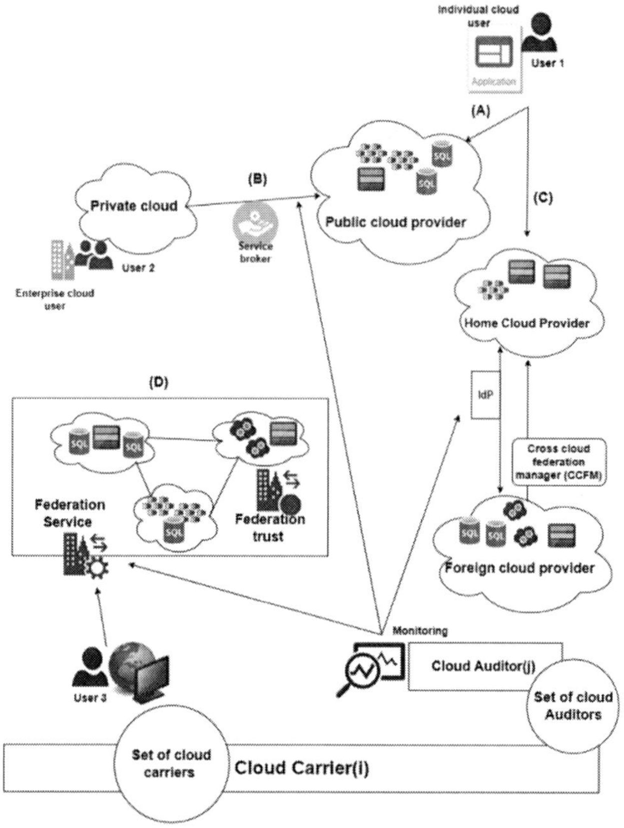

Figure 2: Multiple clouds types entities relationship.

The last two entities are also mentioned in [44]. Different

types of relations control the communication among multiple clouds entities. We use a formula notation to analyze the interactions and relations between various cloud entities under different types of multiple clouds, which facilitates describing the inputs, outputs, and transformations that take place during a specific interaction. Moreover, the formula notation will provide a structured model approach to describe sophisticated scenarios in multiple clouds [42] [44]. The relation depends on a specific application context and the corresponding multiple clouds type deployed. Figure 2: (A, B, C, D) shows the different entities' relationships under different multiple clouds type. A and B describe entities relationship in the multi-cloud with a hybrid deployment model. C illustrates the cross-cloud federation entities relationship, and finally, D represents the federation entities interaction relationship.

The following are the main entities and notations that used in explaining the four main relations depicted in Figure 2.

Main entities: cloud user(s), cloud provider(s), cloud broker(s), middle ware, cloud auditor(s) and cloud carrier(s).

Notation: cloud user i (U_i), cloud provider i (CP_i), relation ij R(ij): U(i) $\implies$ CP(j) a relation from user i to cloud provider j, where $i \in \{1, 2, 3, \ldots, n\}$, $j \in \{1, 2, 3, \ldots, m\}$ and $n, m \in (N)$. N is the set of natural numbers.
It does not necessarily for n and m to be equal due to the cloud multi-tenancy feature [46].

A. Multi-cloud setting: individual user access a public cloud service provider.

Cloud users contact different cloud providers for better services provisioning and extra resources access. They can request various services from various CSPs to satisfy users' demands and needs. **Equation** (1) represents Ri between U_i and CP_j

$$U_i \implies CP_j \tag{1}$$

, where U(i) represent an individual user. Moreover, the SLA controls the communication and the amount of leased resources between cloud users and CSPs. Also, a private cloud that needs extra resources to run its application and better meet its clients' needs can initiate a request to the public cloud. Figure 2: (A) demonstrates user 1 accessing a resource from a public cloud provider using an electronic device.

Trusted entities can be involved to monitor communication as a broker or middleware [45]. Cloud carriers and auditors are applied to assess the service delivery, the privacy and security compliance while supporting the connectivity for the underlying network infrastructure [42]. These have same rules as the single cloud, they can be replicated through the multiple clouds architecture design to behave in a distributed environment and avoid single point of failure. Noted that a cloud provider can serve different users at the same time, meeting a multi-tenancy feature of the cloud [46].

B. Multi-cloud setting: enterprise with its own private cloud access a public cloud service provider.

Users can be an individual working in an organization that holds its own private cloud. However, at specific point of time the private cloud could ask for extra resources or services from a well known cloud vendor, public cloud. This forming a hybrid cloud known as "Cloud Bursting" [37].

Equation (2) represents Rij between CP_i and CP_j.

$$CP_i \implies CP_j \tag{2}$$

However, a cloud provider can serve different users requests at the same time in a sharing and distributed environment maintaining the multi-tenancy feature. Figure 2: (B) shows user 2,the enterprise, running its own private cloud access resources from public cloud.

C. Cross cloud federation.

A cloud provider that lacks resources at specific point of time, home cloud, can dynamically request and get access to the resources from foreign cloud. IdP acts as a trusted point between home and foreign clouds for a secure communication and resource access. A CCFM is another involved trusted party for resource discovery, matching and authentication between the two clouds [1]. The contract for the communication obligation and rules are established dynamically and monitored by the cloud auditor or another motioning technique based on the cloud setting. Cloud auditors assess the service delivery performance and the compliance to the signed agreements. The cloud carrier supports the connectivity for the underlying network infrastructure. Figure 2: (C) shows the entities relationship in a cross-cloud federation where user 1 access can not be satisfied by his/her home cloud. Thus, initiated a dynamic request to foreign cloud that might serve user request. **Equation** (3) represents a dynamic relation denoted by RijD between CP_i (home cloud) and CP_j (foreign cloud) [Cross-cloud federation].

$$CP_i(Home) \implies CP_j(foreign) \quad \text{Dynamic} \tag{3}$$

D. Cloud federation.

In a federated cloud, when a cloud provider has a shortage on it resources and limitation in it underlying infrastructure to run an application, it can statically sign an agreement with another provider to overcome the resource shortage and limitation on its underlying infrastructure [19]–[21], forming a federation.

A cloud broker facilitates collaboration and monitoring across different federation members [43] [45]. Cloud auditors assess the service delivery performance and the compliance to the signed agreements. The cloud carrier supports the connectivity for the underlying network infrastructure.
Figure 2: (D) shows the entities relationship in a cloud federation where user 3 can transparently access different

services offered by federated members.

Users' access can be transparently served by any federation members that statically pre-signed an agreement regulating their communication and service provisioning. **Equation** (4) represents a static relation denoted by RijSt between CP_i and CP_j.

$$CP_i \implies CP_j \qquad \text{Static} \qquad (4)$$

V. Privacy Concerns in Different Types of Multiple Clouds

Privacy concerns become the most critical challenge in multi-cloud while maintaining cloud interoperability. In this section, we will explore the privacy concerns raised by various types of multi-cloud.

A. *Multi-cloud with hybrid deployment model*

Many enterprises with private cloud infrastructure access different services offered from various public cloud providers. The enterprises get many benefits; avoid vendor lock-in with better and cost-effective resource provisioning to their users, greater flexibility, increased efficiency, and more scalability [30] [38]. We assume no trusted parties are deployed with this model as it is difficult to establish and maintain trust and its corresponding relationship in the open, distributed and changing multiple clouds environment. Other privacy challenges include setting the regulations, pre-defined agreements, policies construction, cloud provider commitments, risk management, and ethical behavior towards the involved entities. We focus on user privacy as they are the main actors in the multi-cloud setting. However, the multi-cloud with hybrid deployment model, from our point of view, raises two primary users' privacy concerns:

1) Users' authentication and access privacy.

Users' have to authenticate themselves to access their outsourced data and different services from the public cloud providers. Users can be an individual with their own electronic device, denoted in Section IV by Ri relation, or users can be enterprises with their own private cloud where access are from private cloud to hybrid cloud, denoted in Section IV by Rij.

However, the authentication process reveals user identities, locations, habits and attributes to the cloud provider. There is no guarantee for cloud providers' ethical behavior towards cloud users and their corresponding attributes. Attackers can also monitor user behaviors and access patterns to derive sensitive information about the users and their valuable assets.

In the Cloud-based Vehicular Ad-Hoc Networks (VANET), each sensor node gathers real-time vehicle information and monitors its traffic route—all of this information is outsourced to the cloud to provide different cloud services [75]. Moreover, the sensor nodes can communicate with each other. The communication messages are aggregated to broadcast to a specific group of users in the VANET framework [76]. Through the various forms of communication, each vehicle must independently authenticate itself to sensor nodes to access a particular service. A typical vehicular communication message contains the vehicle's location, direction, and speed. The malicious entity might extract crucial driver information from those communications and use it to impersonate other vehicles identity and deliver false messages that could cause collisions and, at worst, the loss of human lives. Moreover, an intelligent transportation system needs access to the vehicle's location to generate real-time traffic reports and suggest various Points Of Interest (POI) [75] [76]. For such a purpose, driver semantic data for the visited places and current locations had to be extracted. These sensitive details reveal the user's lifestyle and routine. Keeping the privacy of the vehicle or sensor node's identity and information during the communication while enabling each node to authenticate itself privately without disclosing its associated information is cruical in VANET [77].

To sum up, the main privacy concerns in the multi-cloud setting are user authentication and access privacy, which entail identity, attributes, access patterns, and location privacy. These privacy issues are reflected during the vehicle authentication and communication procedure in the cloud-based VANET. Additionally, creating a traffic report in VANET necessitates access to the vehicle's location, which can reveal user habits.

2) Users' data security.

Users' lose control over their outsourced data. If it is transfer in plain format, it will be posed to a different type of disclosure and attacks. Also, it can be easily modified, which affects its integrity and completeness. Encrypted data before outsourcing to maintain its confidentiality adds extra load to the enterprise side, which usually has limited performance capacities and storage space. Moreover, the encryption of the data requires pre-communication between private and public clouds to set private and public keys in the case of public key techniques. More advanced cryptographic techniques (e.g, full homomorphic encryption [57]) are used to encrypt the data to permit operations over the outsource encrypted data.

However, those advanced techniques add extra complexity to the infrastructure which could affect the application usability and performance. Moreover, users' data transferred through other cloud providers could face different policies and access procedures. Another privacy concern is the operation performed by authorized entities over the outsourced data.

Querying the data stored in distributed database cloud storage poses various privacy concerns. We demonstrate query privacy in the multi-cloud genomic application. Many authorized researchers and health organizations query the outsourced encrypted genome data stored in different cloud databases. The query statement searches a cloud database first to meet specific criteria stated in the conditional part of the query and get the result back.

The query details include contents (e.g., conditional part and indices position), outcome, target, and user access pattern. In the context of genomic data, knowing any query contents by unauthorized or malicious entities will reveal sensitive information (e.g., in the genomic sequence, the location of a specific DNA pattern will indicate the type of patient disease). The specific pattern and location detected in the patient determine the classification of the disease in some forms of diabetes, such as Maturity-Onset Diabetes of the Young (MODY) [72]. In [73] [74], they succeeded in securely querying private in genomic datasets to discover which specific genomic alterations are associated with a disease, thus increasing the availability of these valuable datasets. Ensuring the privacy of the query so that the cloud provider will not be able to deduce any information from the query except what is allowed to do, and the researcher will not know any other information on the genomic database. Finally, choosing the most appropriate privacy-preserving techniques that could be applied efficiently, securely, and scalably when inquiring about genomic data is crucial in the genomic domain.

To summarize, user data security entails its confidentiality, integrity, availability, and access rights management, which are other critical privacy concerns in the multi-cloud hybrid deployment model. Moreover, different privacy concerns can be determined based on a specific application context, data sensitivity, application requirements, and entities involved in a particular cloud type.

B. Federated cloud.

1) Horizontal federation architecture.

Cloud providers set pre-defined rules and policies to integrate and establish a federation [1] [19]–[22]. The established regulations, policies, and trust govern the communication between federation members. Users get a wide variety of services from the federation transparently, denoted in Section IV by $RijSt$. However, this type of federation is usually static; if the user wants service outbound to the federation capacities, the user request is denied [1] [19]–[22]. There is also a high possibility of malicious attacks during the members' communication, thus affecting the confidentiality of data and threatening user privacy [47]. Also, there is no guarantee that a subset of federation members collude to extract user-sensitive information.

Moreover, there are many security challenges in constructing a federated cloud [48], which are the longer chain of trust, limited audibility, risk of malicious service components, and liability and legal issues. The users in federated cloud and inter-cloud will face the same privacy concern as those on the multi-cloud hybrid deployment model. Integration of end-to-end security and privacy implementation in the federated cloud is the undergoing research area which is challenging to balance the efficiency and security in the federation implementation [47].

2) Cross-federated cloud and inter-cloud.

When a user wants a service not supported by the cloud provider in which customer is subscribed to and trusted, the cloud provider can collaborate on-fly with another cloud provider to satisfy the user's demands. The corresponding relation denoted in Section IV by $RijD$. The CCFM is the trusted party that starts the resource discovery process till finding the appropriate cloud provider that best matches the request. Ending with the authentication between the home and foreign cloud providers to facilitate the access and resource provisioning processes [1].

The dynamic discovery put the involved entities at high risk in the open and untrusted multiple clouds environment. As there is no pre-defined trust in the dynamic discovery between the cloud providers, maintaining the dynamic trust, in that case, is becoming challenging. Different doubts surrounded trust itself: What is trust? Is it a vulnerability to the system or not? What is the type of trust that could establish? What are the trust requirements and specifications in a dynamic context? What are the relationships between trust, risk, and assurance levels? Is trust enough to guarantee user privacy? What metrics are required to implement a privacy preservation approach in the inter-cloud and cross-federated cloud?

Moreover, identifying the risks will help mitigate undesirable circumstances that threaten user privacy. However, the risk will still depend on a specific context and what is considered valued and require a higher protection mechanism during the dynamic discovery, resource provisioning and access process. Identifying the relationships between trust and risk facilitates dynamic discovery decisions to federate or not [49] [50]. Cross-cloud federation shows its applicability in a wide range of domains starting from research and academia, engineering and construction, financial and industry, real-time data processing, and online gaming [1].

Inter-cloud facilitates the dynamic discovery of the resources in a wider scale domain. Within the federated identity management, user access different federated services and resources. Trust is an essential factor within the federated members to transparently satisfy the user better demands (e.g., a proxy certificate is used for trust implementation in the grid computing [51]).

Single sign-on (SSO) application under inter-cloud enables users to authenticate only once and get access to different web services located at other clouds without the need to be re-authenticated again. Different standard protocols were established in the SSO [52]. The two most popular are Security Assertion Markup Language (SAML 2.0) [53], and OpenID connect [54], each of them with its specifications and format [53] [54]. However, each generates an authentication/access token to delegate the authentication on behalf of the user. The authentication delegation allows access to specific attributes identified in the access token [55]. These protocols should prevent any impersonation and other malicious activities performed by the IdP (e.g., monitoring user access and linking user identities to different activities offered by service providers). Still, securing these protocols against attacks is challenging in web cloud domain. Many attacks are reported [56].

C. The hybrid deployment model under a federated cloud.

Integrating federated cloud with hybrid deployment model known as "Hybrid Federated Cloud Computing," which allows interoperability across different federations. The main objective of this type is to provide an environment with seem-

TABLE I: PRIVACY CONCERNS IN MULTIPLE CLOUDS TYPES.

Cloud type	Deployment model			Privacy concerns	Application
	Public	*Private*	*Hybrid*		
Multi-cloud			✓	• Identity privacy. • Location privacy. • Access pattern privacy. • Query privacy. • Data and access privacy.	• VANET. • Genomic domain.
Federated cloud			✓	• Risk of dynamic discovery. • Authentication privacy. • Access privacy.	Bio-informatic with SSO.
Horizontal federation	✓	✓	✓	• Trust between federation members: – No collude federated members. – longer chain of trust. • Identity privacy. • Risk of malicious service components. • Liability and legal issues. • Limited audibility.	Small organizations.
Cross-federated and inter-cloud			✓	• Identity privacy. • Attribute privacy. • Token access privacy. • Access and authorization privacy.	SSO (SAML 2.0, OIDC protocols)

ingly limitless computational resources, processing power, and storage space that can effectively meet user demands [52] [58]–[61]. In the bio-informatics domain, a bioNimbus [60] [61] is a federated cloud platform in which different independent, heterogenous, private/public/hybrid clouds are collaborated to support other bio-informatics applications. It maintains the internal configuration and privacy policies for each federation member.

BioNimbus supports on-demand resource provisioning in an efficient, flexible, fault tolerance, and scalable way under the hybrid horizontal federation deployment model [60]–[63]. It integrates different bio-informatic workflows for identifying differentially expressed genes in cancer tissue.

Various bio-informatics centers can benefit from the federation collaboration to access other data and have extra storage in a distributed, transparent, and fault tolerance way [62] [64]. The security, including authentication, authorization, and confidentiality, can be implemented in the hybrid federated cloud without adding extra dependency among the federation members through the standard SSO protocols OpenID and OAuth [64]. The user authenticates through their federation provider and gets access to other federation members. The access control list governs the access process based on the federation pre-signed federation agreement.

In [63], they suggest using the attribute-based access control for the bioNimbus operating under a federated cloud, which effectively guarantees that eligible users can only access resources without impacting the authorization response back time. However, when a federation requests additional resources from other public clouds or federations, privacy issues related to authentication and access should be addressed. These issues also include the risk of dynamic discovery and creating a new connection with an unknown federated cloud or cloud provider. Different projects [61] [63] [65]–[71] were implemented for bio-informatics applications under a federation cloud environment. Table I summarizes the privacy concerns within different multiple clouds types concerning various applications.

VI. Conclusion

The main goal of multiple clouds is to maintain cloud interoperability, allowing different clouds to communicate and interact to provide cloud users with a wide variety of resources and high-quality services. Moreover, multiple clouds get around a single cloud architecture limitation by allowing users to access various resources without being stuck to a specific cloud provider. There are different types of multiple clouds: cross-cloud, rain cloud, horizontal federation cloud, and federated cloud. Various applications deploy the cloud type that matches their specifications under public or hybrid deployment models.

Privacy is still of utmost importance in the digital world and has become vital for adopting different kinds of multiple clouds under a specific application domain. The success of multiple clouds adoption and a trustworthy environment is primarily driven by cloud security and preserving cloud users' privacy. The results of the present study's survey provide classifications of multiple clouds types and outline the most common multiple clouds taxonomy. The challenges for public and hybrid deployment models were investigated under different kinds of multiple clouds. For example, the most common concerns under the hybrid deployment model were privacy, security, and trust. However, the relationships that connect single cloud entities no longer suit the multiple clouds architecture; thus, for the purposes of the present study, the relationships were extended from a single cloud to behave under different kinds of multiple clouds in a distributed manner. As privacy is a key consideration when deploying multiple clouds, the study introduced different privacy concerns in various applications that deploy a specific type of multiple clouds.

For example, the bio-informatic domain deploys a hybrid federated cloud, which raises authentication and access privacy concerns. Also, an SSO web application that deploys a cross-federated cloud will pose token access privacy, identity, and attributes privacy. The privacy concerns outlined in the study underscore the need to examine more applications that use multiple clouds and show the current solutions for handling these privacy issues. Moreover, a supplementary survey should explore the potential of developing new techniques for privacy preservation in multiple clouds.

Acknowledgments: We acknowledge the support of the Natural Sciences and Engineering Research Council of Canada (NSERC [funding reference number 03181]). We also acknowledge the input from Dr. Mahdi Daghmehchi Firoozjaei, School of Computer Science, University of Windsor.

REFERENCES

[1] U. Ahmed, I. Raza, and S. A. Hussain, "Trust evaluation in cross-cloud federation: Survey and requirement analysis," ACM Computing Surveys, vol. 52, no. 1. Association for Computing Machinery, Feb. 01, 2019. doi: 10.1145/3292499.

[2] B. Varghese, N. Wang, S. Barbhuiya, P. Kilpatrick, and D. S. Nikolopoulos, "Challenges and Opportunities in Edge Computing," in Proceedings - 2016 IEEE International Conference on Smart Cloud, SmartCloud 2016, Dec. 2016, pp. 20–26. doi: 10.1109/SmartCloud.2016.18.

[3] D. Bernstein, E. Ludvigson, K. Sankar, S. Diamond, and M. Morrow, "Blueprint for the intercloud - Protocols and formats for cloud computing interoperability," in Proceedings of the 2009 4th International Conference on Internet and Web Applications and Services, ICIW 2009, 2009, pp. 328–336. doi: 10.1109/ICIW.2009.55.

[4] K. Keahey, M. Tsugawa, A. Matsunaga, and J. Fortes, "Sky computing," IEEE Internet Comput, vol. 13, no. 5, pp. 43–51, 2009, doi: 10.1109/MIC.2009.94.

[5] S. Shetty, A. P. Manu, V. Kumar, and C. Antony, "Need of Multi-Cloud Environment and Related Issues: A Survey," Journal of Xian University of Architecture & Technology, vol. 12, pp. 78-87, 2020.

[6] A. Celesti, F. Tusa, M. Villari, and A. Puliafito, "How to enhance cloud architectures to enable cross-federation," in Proceedings - 2010 IEEE 3rd International Conference on Cloud Computing, CLOUD 2010, 2010, pp. 337–345. doi: 10.1109/CLOUD.2010.46.

[7] S. Subashini and V. Kavitha, "A survey on security issues in service delivery models of cloud computing," Journal of Network and Computer Applications, vol. 34, no. 1. pp. 1–11, Jan. 2011. doi: 10.1016/j.jnca.2010.07.006.

[8] "Computer Communications and Networks." [Online]. Available: http://www.springer.com/series/4198. Accessed: March 2, 2023.

[9] M. A. AlZain, E. Pardede, B. Soh, and J. A. Thom, "Cloud computing security: From single to multi-clouds," in Proceedings of the Annual Hawaii International Conference on System Sciences, 2012, pp. 5490–5499. doi: 10.1109/HICSS.2012.153.

[10] N. Thillaiarasu and S. Chenthurpandian, "Enforcing security and privacy over multi-cloud framework using assessment techniques," in Proceedings of the 10th International Conference on Intelligent Systems and Control, ISCO 2016, Oct. 2016. pp. 1-6, doi: 10.1109/ISCO.2016.7727001.

[11] Y. Elkhatib, "Mapping cross-cloud systems: Challenges and opportunities," in 8th USENIX Workshop on Hot Topics in Cloud Computing (HotCloud 16), pp. 1-5, 2016.

[12] N. Grozev and R. Buyya, "Inter-Cloud architectures and application brokering: Taxonomy and survey," Softw Pract Exp, vol. 44, no. 3, pp. 369–390, Mar. 2014, doi: 10.1002/spe.2168.

[13] A. N. Toosi, R. N. Calheiros, and R. Buyya, "Interconnected cloud computing environments: Challenges, taxonomy, and survey," ACM Computing Surveys (CSUR), vol. 47, no. 1, pp. 1-47, 2014.

[14] M. R. M. Assis and L. F. Bittencourt, "A survey on cloud federation architectures: Identifying functional and non-functional properties," Journal of Network and Computer Applications, vol. 72. Academic Press, pp. 51–71, Sep. 01, 2016. doi: 10.1016/j.jnca.2016.06.014.

[15] D. Gurusamy and T. K. Elemo, "Direct-cloud, multi-cloud, and connected-cloud – terminologies make a move in cloud computing," International Journal of Innovative Technology and Exploring Engineering, vol. 8, no. 9 Special Issue 2, pp. 386–393, Jul. 2019, doi: 10.35940/ijitee.I1083.0789S219.

[16] J. Hong, T. Dreibholz, J. A. Schenkel, and J. A. Hu, "An Overview of Multi-cloud Computing," in Advances in Intelligent Systems and Computing, 2019, vol. 927, pp. 1055–1068. doi: 10.1007/978-3-030-15035-8-103.

[17] S. Kathuria, 'A survey on security provided by multi-clouds in cloud computing', International Journal of Scientific Research in Network Security and Communication, vol. 6, no. 1, pp. 23–27, 2018.

[18] D. Petcu, 'Multi-cloud: expectations and current approaches', in Proceedings of the 2013 international workshop on Multi-cloud applications and federated clouds, 2013, pp. 1–6.

[19] L. Chouhan, P. Bansal, B. Lauhny, and Y. Chaudhary, "A Survey on Cloud Federation Architecture and Challenges," in Lecture Notes in Networks and Systems, vol. 100, Springer, 2020, pp. 51–65. doi: 10.1007/978-981-15-2071-6-5.

[20] R. Buyya, J. Broberg, and A. M. Goscinski, Cloud computing: Principles and paradigms. John Wiley and Sons, 2010, pp. 393-410

[21] J. Hong, T. Dreibholz, J. A. Schenkel, and J. A. Hu, "An Overview of Multi-cloud Computing," in Advances in Intelligent Systems and Computing, 2019, vol. 927, pp. 1055–1068. doi: 10.1007/978-3-030-15035-8-103.

[22] B. Fabian, T. Ermakova, and P. Junghanns, "Collaborative and secure sharing of healthcare data in multi-clouds," Information Systems, vol. 48, pp. 132-150, 2015.

[23] M. R. M. Assis, L. F. Bittencourt, and R. Tolosana-Calasanz, "Cloud federation: Characterization and conceptual model," in Proceedings - 2014 IEEE/ACM 7th International Conference on Utility and Cloud Computing, UCC 2014, Jan. 2014, pp. 585–590. doi: 10.1109/UCC.2014.90.

[24] T. Kurze, M. Klems, D. Bermbach, A. Lenk, S. Tai, and M. Kunze, 'Cloud federation', Cloud Computing, vol. 2011, pp. 32–38, 2011.

[25] L. Mashayekhy, M. M. Nejad, and D. Grosu, "A Trust-Aware Mechanism for Cloud Federation Formation," IEEE Transactions on Cloud Computing, vol. 9, no. 4, pp. 1278–1292, 2021, doi: 10.1109/TCC.2019.2911831.

[26] D. Villegas et al., "Cloud federation in a layered service model," in Journal of Computer and System Sciences, 2012, vol. 78, no. 5, pp. 1330–1344. doi: 10.1016/j.jcss.2011.12.017.

[27] M. A. Salehi, A. N. Toosi, and R. Buyya, "Contention management in federated virtualized distributed systems: implementation and evaluation," Software: Practice and Experience, vol. 44, no. 3, pp. 353-368, Mar. 2014.

[28] H. A. Imran et al., 'Multi-cloud: a comprehensive review', in 2020 IEEE 23rd International Multitopic Conference (INMIC), 2020, pp. 1–5.

[29] A. N. Toosi, R. N. Calheiros, R. K. Thulasiram, and R. Buyya, "Resource provisioning policies to increase IaaS provider's profit in a federated cloud environment," in Proc.- 2011 IEEE International Conference on HPCC 2011, pp. 279–287. doi: 10.1109/HPCC.2011.44.

[30] M. Singhal, S. Chandrasekhar, T. Ge, R. Sandhu, R. Krishnan, G. J. Ahn, and E. Bertino, "Collaboration in multicloud computing environments: Framework and security issues," Computer, vol. 46, no. 2, pp. 76-84, Feb. 2013.

[31] T. Diaby and B. B. Rad, "Cloud Computing: A review of the Concepts and Deployment Models," International Journal of Information Technology and Computer Science, vol. 9, no. 6, pp. 50–58, Jun. 2017, doi: 10.5815/ijitcs.2017.06.07.

[32] L. Savu, "Cloud computing: Deployment models, delivery models, risks and research challanges," in 2011 International Conference on Computer and Management, CAMAN 2011, 2011. doi: 10.1109/CAMAN.2011.5778816.

[33] W. Jansen and T. Grance, "Guidelines on security and privacy in public cloud computing," Gaithersburg, MD, 2011. doi: 10.6028/NIST.SP.800-144.

[34] P. Hofmann and D. Woods, "Cloud computing: The limits of public clouds for business applications," IEEE Internet Comput, vol. 14, no. 6, pp. 90–93, Nov. 2010, doi: 10.1109/MIC.2010.136.

[35] K. Ren, C. Wang, and Q. Wang, "Security challenges for the public cloud," IEEE Internet Computing, vol. 16, no. 1. pp. 69–73, Jan. 2012. doi: 10.1109/MIC.2012.14.

[36] S. Islam, M. Ouedraogo, C. Kalloniatis, H. Mouratidis, and S. Gritzalis, "Assurance of Security and Privacy Requirements for Cloud Deployment

Models," IEEE Transactions on Cloud Computing, vol. 6, no. 2, pp. 387–400, Apr. 2018, doi: 10.1109/TCC.2015.2511719.

[37] T. Guo, U. Sharma, P. Shenoy, T. Wood, and S. Sahu, "Cost-aware cloud bursting for enterprise applications," in ACM Transactions on Internet Technology, 2014, vol. 13, no. 3. doi: 10.1145/2602571.

[38] V. Viji Rajendran and S. Swamynathan, "Hybrid model for dynamic evaluation of trust in cloud services," Wireless Networks, vol. 22, no. 6, pp. 1807–1818, Aug. 2016, doi: 10.1007/s11276-015-1069-y.

[39] J. Abawajy, 'Establishing trust in hybrid cloud computing environments', in 2011IEEE 10th International Conference on Trust, Security and Privacy in Computing and Communications, 2011, pp. 118–125.

[40] C. Lin and V. Varadharajan, 'A hybrid trust model for enhancing security in distributed systems', in The Second International Conference on Availability, Reliability and Security (ARES'07), 2007, pp. 35–42.

[41] A. Marinos and G. Briscoe, 'Community cloud computing', in Cloud Computing: First International Conference, CloudCom 2009, Beijing, China, December 1-4, 2009. Proceedings 1, 2009, pp. 472–484.

[42] F. Liu et al., 'NIST cloud computing reference architecture', NIST special publication, vol. 500, no. 2011, pp. 1–28, 2011.

[43] A. Elhabbash, F. Samreen, J. Hadley, and Y. Elkhatib, "Cloud brokerage: A systematic survey," ACM Computing Surveys, vol. 51, no. 6. Association for Computing Machinery, Jan. 01, 2019. doi: 10.1145/3274657.

[44] A. Ghorbel, M. Ghorbel, and M. Jmaiel, 'Privacy in cloud computing environments: a survey and research challenges', The Journal of Supercomputing, vol. 73, no. 6, pp. 2763–2800, 2017.

[45] T. Halabi and M. Bellaiche, "A broker-based framework for standardization and management of Cloud Security-SLAs," Comput Secur, vol. 75, pp. 59–71, Jun. 2018, doi: 10.1016/j.cose.2018.01.019.

[46] H. AlJahdali, A. Albatli, P. Garraghan, P. Townend, L. Lau, and J. Xu, 'Multi-tenancy in cloud computing', in 2014 IEEE 8th international symposium on service oriented system engineering, 2014, pp. 344–351.

[47] R. Kumar, S. · Jitendra, A. · Sanjeev, S. · Narendra, S. Chaudhari, and · K K Shukla Editors, "Lecture Notes in Networks and Systems 100." [Online]. Available: http://www.springer.com/series/15179

[48] K. Bernsmed, M. G. Jaatun, P. H. Meland, and A. Undheim, "Thunder in the Clouds: Security challenges and solutions for federated Clouds," in CloudCom 2012 - Proceedings: 2012 4th IEEE International Conference on Cloud Computing Technology and Science, 2012, pp. 113–120. doi: 10.1109/CloudCom.2012.6427547.

[49] P. Arias Cabarcos, F. Almenárez, F. Gómez Mármol, and A. Marín, "To federate or not to federate: A reputation-based mechanism to dynamize cooperation in identity management," Wirel Pers Commun, vol. 75, no. 3, pp. 1769–1786, Apr. 2014, doi: 10.1007/s11277-013-1338-y.

[50] P. Arias-Cabarcos, F. A. Rez-Mendoza, A. Marín-López, D. Díaz-Sánchez, and R. Sánchez-Guerrero, "A metric-based approach to assess risk for 'On cloud' federated identity management," Journal of Network and Systems Management, vol. 20, no. 4, pp. 513–533, Dec. 2012, doi: 10.1007/s10922-012-9244-2.

[51] M. Ogawa and L. Xin, "Proxy Certificate Trust List for Grid Computing Time-Sensitive Pushdown Systems View project Proxy Certificate Trust List for Grid Computing." [Online]. Available: https://www.researchgate.net/publication/252163600. Accessed: March 2, 2023.

[52] V. Radha and D. H. Reddy, "A Survey on Single Sign-On Techniques," Procedia Technology, vol. 4, pp. 134–139, 2012, doi: 10.1016/j.protcy.2012.05.019.

[53] E. Maler et al., 'Security and privacy considerations for the oasis security assertion markup language (saml) v2. 0', Language (SAML), vol. 2, p. 0, 2005.

[54] C. Mainka, V. Mladenov, J. Schwenk, and T. Wich, "SoK: Single Sign-On Security - An Evaluation of OpenID Connect," in Proceedings - 2nd IEEE European Symposium on Security and Privacy, EuroS and P 2017, Jun. 2017, pp. 251–266. doi: 10.1109/EuroSP.2017.32.

[55] H. Gomi, "Dynamic identity delegation using access tokens in federated environments," in Proceedings - 2011 IEEE 9th International Conference on Web Services, ICWS 2011, 2011, pp. 612–619. doi: 10.1109/ICWS.2011.30.

[56] M. Ghasemisharif, A. Ramesh, S. Checkoway, C. Kanich, J. Polakis, and A. Ramesh, Open access to the Proceedings of the 27th USENIX Security Symposium is sponsored by USENIX. O Single Sign-Off, Where Art Thou? An Empirical Analysis of Single Sign-On Account Hijacking and Session Management on the Web O Single Sign-Off.

[57] C. Gentry, A fully homomorphic encryption scheme. Stanford university, 2009.

[58] R. Gallon, M. Holanda, A. Araújo, and M. E. Walter, 'Storage policy for genomic data in hybrid federated clouds', in Advances in Bioinformatics and Computational Biology: 9th Brazilian Symposium on Bioinformatics, BSB 2014, Belo Horizonte, Brazil, October 28-30, 2014, Proceedings 9, 2014, pp. 107–114.

[59] M. Rosa et al., "BioNimbuZ: A federated cloud platform for bioinformatics applications," in Proceedings - 2016 IEEE International Conference on Bioinformatics and Biomedicine, BIBM 2016, Jan. 2017, pp. 548–555. doi: 10.1109/BIBM.2016.7822580.

[60] C. A. L. Borges, H. v. Saldanha, E. Ribeiro, M. T. Holanda, A. P. F. Araujo, and M. E. M. T. Walter, "Task scheduling in a federated cloud infrastructure for bioinformatics applications," in CLOSER 2012 - Proceedings of the 2nd International Conference on Cloud Computing and Services Science, 2012, pp. 114–120. doi: 10.5220/0003932801140120.

[61] A. P. Heath et al., "Bionimbus: A cloud for managing, analyzing and sharing large genomics datasets," Journal of the American Medical Informatics Association, vol. 21, no. 6, pp. 969–975, Jan. 2014, doi: 10.1136/amiajnl-2013-002155.

[62] D. Lima et al., "A storage policy for a hybrid federated cloud platform: A case study for bioinformatics," in Proceedings - 14th IEEE/ACM International Symposium on Cluster, Cloud, and Grid Computing, CCGrid 2014, 2014, pp. 738–747. doi: 10.1109/CCGrid.2014.102.

[63] H. H. D. P. M. Costa, A. P. F. de Araújo, J. J. C. Gondim, M. T. de Holanda, and M. E. M. T. Walter, "Attribute based access control in federated clouds: A case study in bioinformatics," in 2017 12th Iberian Conference on Information Systems and Technologies (CISTI), pp. 1-7, June 2017.

[64] H. Saldanha et al., "Towards a Hybrid Federated Cloud Platform to Efficiently Execute Bioinformatics Workflows," in Bioinformatics, InTech, 2012. doi: 10.5772/50289.

[65] B. Langmead, K. D. Hansen, and J. T. Leek, "Cloud-scale RNA-sequencing differential expression analysis with Myrna," 2010. [Online]. Available: http://genomebiology.com/content/11/8/R83

[66] C. Hoffa et al., "On the use of cloud computing for scientific workflows," in Proceedings - 4th IEEE International Conference on eScience, eScience 2008, 2008, pp. 640–645. doi: 10.1109/eScience.2008.167.

[67] D. P. Wall, P. Kudtarkar, V. A. Fusaro, R. Pivovarov, P. Patil, and P. J. Tonellato, "Cloud computing for comparative genomics," 2010. [Online]. Available: http://www.biomedcentral.com/1471-2105/11/259

[68] R. Li et al., "SNP detection for massively parallel whole-genome resequencing," Genome Res, vol. 19, no. 6, pp. 1124–1132, Jun. 2009, doi: 10.1101/gr.088013.108.

[69] B. Pratt, J. J. Howbert, N. I. Tasman, and E. J. Nilsson, "Mr-Tandem: Parallel x!Tandem using Hadoop MapReduce on Amazon web services," Bioinformatics, vol. 28, no. 1, pp. 136–137, Jan. 2012, doi: 10.1093/bioinformatics/btr615.

[70] L. Zhang, S. Gu, Y. Liu, B. Wang, and F. Azuaje, "Gene set analysis in the cloud," Bioinformatics, vol. 28, no. 2, pp. 294–295, Jan. 2012, doi: 10.1093/bioinformatics/btr630.

[71] B. Lang, I. Foster, F. Siebenlist, R. Ananthakrishnan, and T. Freeman, "A flexible attribute based access control method for grid computing," J Grid Comput, vol. 7, no. 2, pp. 169–180, 2009, doi: 10.1007/s10723-008-9112-1.

[72] M. Najam, R. U. Rasool, H. F. Ahmad, U. Ashraf, and A. W. Malik, "Pattern Matching for DNA Sequencing Data Using Multiple Bloom Filters," Biomed Res Int, vol. 2019, 2019, doi: 10.1155/2019/7074387

[73] M. Akgün, A. O. Bayrak, B. Ozer, and M. Ş. Sağiroğlu, "Privacy preserving processing of genomic data: A survey," Journal of Biomedical Informatics, vol. 56. Academic Press Inc., pp. 103–111, Aug. 01, 2015. doi: 10.1016/j.jbi.2015.05.022

[74] S. Simmons, C. Sahinalp, and B. Berger, "Enabling Privacy-Preserving GWASs in Heterogeneous Human Populations," Cell Syst, vol. 3, no. 1, pp. 54–61, Jul. 2016, doi: 10.1016/j.cels.2016.04.013.

[75] S. Sharma and A. Kaul, "A survey on Intrusion Detection Systems and Honeypot based proactive security mechanisms in VANETs and VANET Cloud," Vehicular Communications, vol. 12. Elsevier Inc., pp. 138–164, Apr. 01, 2018.

[76] K. Sarwar, S. Yongchareon, J. Yu, and S. Ur Rehman, "A Survey on Privacy Preservation in Fog-Enabled Internet of Things," ACM Comput Surv, vol. 55, no. 1, pp. 1–39, Jan. 2023, doi: 10.1145/3474554.

[77] I. Ali, A. Hassan, and F. Li, "Authentication and privacy schemes for vehicular ad hoc networks (VANETs): A survey," Vehicular Communications, vol. 16. Elsevier Inc., pp. 45–61, Apr. 01, 2019. doi: 10.1016/j.vehcom.2019.02.002.

Challenges and Solutions in IoT Security: A Cross-Industry Perspective

Ibrahim El-Shekeil
ibrahim.el-shekeil@metrostate.edu

Thomas Mullins
thomas.mullins@my.metrostate.edu

Tariq Haji Hassan
tariq.hajihassan@my.metrostate.edu

Jet Lao
jet.lao@my.metrostate.edu

Xuezeng Yang
xuezeng.yang@my.metrostate.edu

Computer Science and Cybersecurity, Metro State University
700 East Seventh Street, Saint Paul, Minnesota 55106, USA

***Abstract*—In the age of rapid technological advancements, the Internet of Things (IoT) has emerged as a revolutionary paradigm, transforming various industries such as healthcare, agriculture, transportation, smart homes, and smart cities. IoT technology has the potential to revolutionize our daily lives, enabling remote monitoring, personalized treatment, real-time data analysis, and improving the overall efficiency and sustainability of these sectors. However, the increasing use and dependence on IoT devices has raised significant concerns regarding security, privacy, and ethical implications. This paper provides a comprehensive overview of IoT security challenges, examines the role of government standards and regulations, and explores case studies that demonstrate the practical implications of IoT security in various industries. Furthermore, the paper discusses comprehensive solutions to overcome IoT security limitations and challenges, emphasizing the importance of education and awareness, collaboration between stakeholders, and the development of robust security protocols. By understanding and addressing these challenges, stakeholders can ensure the safe and responsible use of IoT devices, maximize their benefits, and minimize potential risks.**

***Keywords*—Internet of Things (IoT); Privacy concerns; Government standards; Cyber-attacks; IoT Security.**

I. Introduction

The IoT is transforming industries such as healthcare, agriculture, and transportation through connected devices that collect and exchange data, leading to enhanced efficiency, productivity, and decision-making [5]. However, the widespread adoption of IoT technologies introduces significant challenges concerning security, privacy, and trust, as these interconnected devices can be susceptible to cyber-attacks, data breaches, and unauthorized access.

The integration of cloud and edge computing within the IoT ecosystem has bolstered the system's capacity to handle large data volumes. Cloud computing provides robust infrastructure and offloading capabilities, while edge computing brings data processing closer to the source, thereby reducing transmission needs and potential data vulnerabilities [19], [29]. Yet, this integration is not without its challenges. Centralized data processing and storage in cloud computing can lead to security issues and single points of failure, while ensuring the security and reliability of distributed resources in edge computing presents its own set of obstacles [40].

In this paper, we explore the challenges associated with IoT, including security and privacy, and discuss potential solutions. We present case studies illustrating IoT applications in various sectors and explore hypothetical implementation scenarios to highlight potential pitfalls and strategies for overcoming them.

The rest of the paper is organized as follows: Section II addresses the challenges and limitations of IoT security. Section III explores the role of governmental standards in mitigating these challenges. Section IV presents case studies from various sectors. Section V discusses comprehensive solutions to IoT security limitations. Finally, in Section VI, we summarize the key findings and emphasize the need for continued efforts in IoT security to realize the full potential of this technology.

II. Current Limitations and Challenges of IoT

The IoT has experienced rapid growth and development in recent years. Despite the numerous benefits and innovations that IoT brings to various industries, it is still faced with several limitations and challenges that need to be addressed. In this section, we will discuss the current limitations and challenges in IoT technology. These encompass a range of concerns, including security, interoperability, privacy, resource constraints including energy efficiency, and legal, regulatory, and standardization issues. Each of these areas presents unique challenges but they are also interconnected, contributing to a complex landscape that must be navigated to fully realize the potential of IoT.

A. Security Challenges

One of the primary concerns in IoT is the security of connected devices. The vast network of connected devices presents numerous vulnerabilities that can be exploited by malicious actors. The lack of standardization in IoT security protocols, combined with the increasing number of devices, makes it difficult to ensure the security of every device in the ecosystem [15]. Recent studies have highlighted various security challenges in IoT, such as data breaches, malware attacks, and unauthorized access [20]. These security threats not only compromise sensitive information but can also cause significant disruptions in the operation of IoT devices and systems.

B. Interoperability Issues

The multitude of manufacturers in the IoT domain, each producing devices with unique hardware and software specifications, contributes to a significant challenge: interoperability. The diversity in these devices can inhibit seamless communication, causing inefficiencies in the larger system. This situation is further compounded by a lack of standardized IoT communication protocols, making it even more difficult for devices to work together and share data effectively, thus potentially compromising overall performance. To address these interoperability challenges, it's necessary to foster the development and adoption of standardized communication protocols. Moreover, integrating a unified IoT framework could facilitate interoperability across the extensive range of IoT devices [26].

C. Privacy Concerns

Privacy in IoT systems is a growing concern due to the volume and sensitivity of data collected and processed by these devices. Many IoT devices have insufficient security mechanisms, leaving them vulnerable to unauthorized access and data breaches, which can compromise users' privacy [22].

One specific example of a privacy concern in the IoT field is the security of electronic health records (EHR) stored in the cloud. Access to these records needs to be controlled to protect sensitive personal information. In response to this challenge, researchers have proposed privacy-preserving access control schemes, such as the one suggested by Ming and Zhang, which provides fine-grained access control for EHR data stored in the cloud, preserving the privacy of the EHR owner [24].

In summary, privacy concerns in IoT systems are multi-faceted, and addressing these concerns requires the development and implementation of robust security measures. More work is needed to protect user privacy in the rapidly evolving IoT landscape [22].

D. Scalability, Resource Constraints, and Energy Efficiency

A significant challenge in IoT is the scalability of the network as the number of connected devices continues to grow exponentially. Managing and processing the massive amounts of data generated by these devices requires considerable computational and storage resources [10].

In addition, IoT devices often have limited processing power, memory, and battery life, which further complicates the scalability of IoT networks [32]. The energy consumption of IoT devices is a notable challenge, particularly as many of these devices are powered by batteries with limited lifespans. IoT devices have varying power requirements, with those demanding higher power rapidly draining batteries, requiring frequent replacements [37].

This issue becomes especially challenging for devices installed in hard-to-reach locations or those that necessitate constant monitoring [4]. The limited battery life of IoT devices can also hinder their effectiveness in critical applications, such as healthcare and transportation, where continuous monitoring is essential [31].

Addressing these intertwined challenges requires the development of efficient data processing and communication techniques, such as edge computing and fog computing, which enable data processing closer to the devices, reducing the load on the central network [36]. Furthermore, adopting energy-efficient protocols and algorithms can help mitigate the resource constraints of IoT devices, allowing for more sustainable and scalable networks.

E. Legal, Regulatory, and Standardization Challenges

The rapid expansion of IoT has led to various legal and regulatory challenges, as well as issues concerning the lack of clear standards. As IoT devices collect, store, and process vast amounts of data, they often intersect with existing regulations, such as data protection laws and cybersecurity requirements [23].

One significant challenge is the integration of blockchain technologies with IoT in sectors like healthcare, where compliance with healthcare regulatory organizations such as HIPAA and GDPR is paramount. For instance, the principle of immutability of blockchain clashes with the right to be forgotten principle under GDPR, creating regulatory challenges in such integrations [23].

Furthermore, the global nature of IoT networks raises questions about jurisdiction and the applicability of national laws to cross-border data flows [14].

The absence of standards and regulations for IoT devices is a significant limitation. The lack of clear regulations and standards can make it difficult to ensure the security and privacy of users' data [21], [22]. Furthermore, the lack of standardization and interoperability between different devices and systems can restrict the technology's potential and effectiveness [20].

Addressing the legal, regulatory, and standardization challenges in IoT requires a coordinated effort among policy-makers, industry stakeholders, and researchers. This joint effort aims to develop comprehensive legal frameworks and standards that account for the unique characteristics of IoT systems. These frameworks should balance the need for innovation and growth with the protection of users' rights and interests, thereby ensuring the safe and responsible development of IoT technology [34].

F. Challenges of IoT Security: An Interconnected View

As we examine the distinct challenges and limitations associated with IoT security, it is paramount to acknowledge the interconnected nature of these issues. Each of the challenges we've dissected—encompassing privacy and data protection, lack of standardization, energy constraints, and legal, regulatory, and standardization challenges—does not exist in isolation. Rather, they form an intricate web of obstacles that collectively shape the IoT security landscape.

TABLE I. INTERCONNECTED CHALLENGES IN IOT SECURITY

Challenge	Interconnection	Impact on IoT Security
Privacy and Data Protection	Tied to standardization and resource constraints	Privacy breaches due to lack of uniform security measures and energy constraints
Lack of Standardization	Links to privacy concerns, resource constraints, and regulatory issues	Inconsistent security features across devices, potential privacy issues, and challenges in implementing energy-efficient solutions
Resource Constraints	Influences privacy, standardization, and cost-effectiveness	Limited adoption of energy-efficient security solutions due to power constraints and cost considerations
Legal, Regulatory, and Standardization Issues	Directly related to privacy, standardization, and cost-effectiveness	Legal and compliance challenges may affect the adoption and implementation of consistent security and privacy measures

The privacy concerns tie directly into the lack of standardized protocols and regulations in the IoT industry. The absence of a unified regulatory framework leads to disparate security measures across devices and systems, thus compromising data integrity and user privacy. The energy constraints, as well as the scarcity of resources in IoT devices, further exacerbate these issues.

The interconnectedness of challenges also highlights that the legal and regulatory aspects cannot be separated from technological and standardization efforts. Legal frameworks need to evolve concurrently with technology to effectively address privacy, security, and interoperability challenges.

This interconnectedness of challenges also means that the strategies employed to address them cannot be piecemeal. A comprehensive, holistic approach is required—one that recognizes these challenges as parts of a larger, complex system rather than separate problems to be solved independently. It underscores the need for collaborative efforts across the industry, spanning policy-makers, manufacturers, service providers, and end-users.

Only through such a comprehensive and collaborative approach can we begin to untangle this complex web of challenges and forge a path towards a secure, robust, and efficient IoT ecosystem. This understanding informs the solutions and recommendations we discuss in the next section, emphasizing the importance of a concerted and coordinated response to the multifaceted challenges of IoT security.

Figure 1 illustrates the interlinked nature of IoT challenges. Security sits at the heart of this matrix, emphasizing its crucial role. Other challenges are directly tied to security, stressing their impact on it. The double arrows ($\rightleftarrows$) denote the reciprocal relationship among these challenges.

For example, scalability concerns can exacerbate security issues, with an increased number of devices implying a broader attack surface. Conversely, security challenges could hamper scalability, as a system with compromised security might face difficulties in scaling efficiently due to the need for enhanced security controls.

This representation underscores that improving IoT security isn't a standalone mission but rather involves addressing intertwined challenges collectively and coherently.

Table I details each main challenge, its interconnections with other challenges, and the overall impact these links have on IoT security. The connections are demonstrative and not exhaustive, illustrating the need for a holistic approach to address the complex landscape of IoT security challenges.

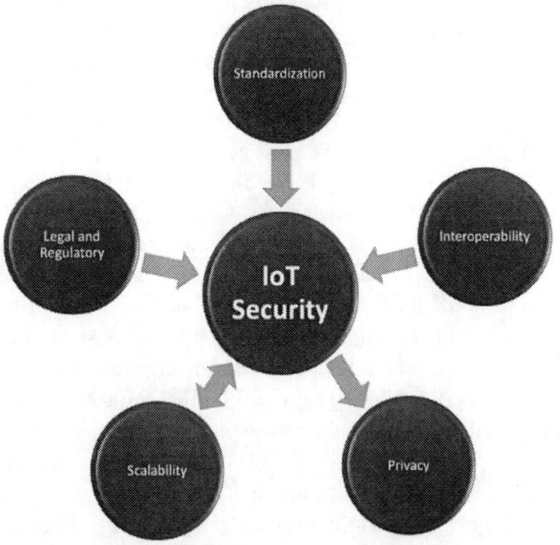

FIG. 1. INTERCONNECTED CHALLENGES IN IOT SECURITY

In summary, addressing the present limitations and challenges of IoT is crucial to ensure the continued evolution and success of this technology. By developing standardized security protocols, we can tackle interoperability and privacy issues. The adoption of robust energy-efficient strategies and resource management methods can optimize the IoT networks' performance, considering the constraints of IoT devices. By addressing the intertwining issues of legalities, regulations, and standardization, we can create a more secure and seamless environment for IoT to thrive. As such, by acknowledging the interconnected nature of these challenges and working towards a comprehensive and collaborative approach, IoT has the potential to overcome these obstacles and continue to drive innovation across industries, enhancing the quality of life for users.

III. GOVERNMENT STANDARDS

Governments around the world are recognizing the importance of IoT and the potential risks associated with its use. As a result, several initiatives have been launched to develop standards and regulations to ensure the safe and responsible use of IoT devices. These initiatives aim to provide guidance to manufacturers and users of IoT devices and to promote interoperability and security across different devices and platforms [30].

One such initiative is the National Institute of Standards and Technology (NIST) Cybersecurity Framework, developed by the US Department of Commerce [38]. The framework provides a set of guidelines and best practices for managing cybersecurity risk for IoT devices. It includes five core functions: identify, protect, detect, respond, and recover. Each function includes a set of categories and subcategories that provide guidance for managing cybersecurity risk. The framework has been widely adopted by organizations in various industries, including healthcare, finance, and energy.

In addition to the NIST framework, several other government initiatives have been launched to develop standards and regulations for IoT devices. The European Union (EU) has developed the General Data Protection Regulation (GDPR), which aims to protect the privacy and security of personal data [27]. The GDPR applies to all organizations that process personal data of EU residents, regardless of their location. The regulation includes several requirements, such as the need for explicit consent for data processing, the right to access and delete personal data, and mandatory data breach reporting.

Similarly, the International Organization for Standardization (ISO) has developed several standards for IoT devices, including ISO/IEC 27001 [12] and ISO/IEC 27002 [13], which provide guidelines for information security management. More recently, ISO/IEC 21823-1:2019 [11] provides guidance on the interoperability of IoT devices and systems.

While government initiatives are essential for promoting the safe and responsible use of IoT devices, there are also limitations to these initiatives. One limitation is the lack of global standards and regulations, which can lead to inconsistencies and fragmentation in the IoT market. Another limitation is the slow pace of regulation development, which can lag behind the rapid pace of technological innovation. Additionally, regulations can also be limited by their enforcement mechanisms, as some regulations lack the teeth needed to ensure compliance and accountability [9].

Despite these limitations, government standards and regulations are crucial for ensuring the safe and responsible use of IoT devices. They provide guidance for manufacturers and users of IoT devices, promote interoperability and security, and protect the privacy and security of personal data.

IV. Case Studies on the Security of Internet of Things Devices

The pervasive adoption of connected devices in various sectors, including healthcare, agriculture, transportation, smart homes, and smart cities, underscores the increasing importance of security and privacy. In this section, we will reference actual case studies that illustrate real security issues in these industries. Additionally, we will present *hypothetical real-world implementation scenarios*. While these scenarios are conjectural, they are designed to reflect plausible situations and serve as illustrative examples to shed light on the potential challenges and limitations of IoT security.

A. Case Study 1: Smart Home Technology

Smart home technology refers to the use of connected devices to automate and control various aspects of the home, including lighting, temperature, security, and entertainment. One example of smart home technology implementation is the Nest Learning Thermostat. This device learns user preferences and adjusts the temperature accordingly, resulting in up to 20% energy savings [3]. Another example is the Amazon Echo, a voice-controlled assistant that can control smart devices, play music, and answer questions.

While smart home technology offers several benefits, including convenience, energy efficiency, and increased security, there are challenges associated with its implementation. One major challenge is the lack of standardization and interoperability. Different devices use different protocols and communication standards, making it difficult to integrate them into a single system [1]. Additionally, the security of these devices is a concern, as they can be vulnerable to hacking and data breaches [4].

Hypothetical Implementation Scenario: To illustrate the deployment of IoT in the context of smart homes, let's hypothetically consider a smart home security system. This system could comprise various IoT devices like security cameras, motion detectors, and smart locks, all interconnected through a centralized hub. A user could then remotely monitor and manage these devices using a mobile application, thus enhancing the ease and efficiency of home security management.

Let's assume a homeowner in California, USA, decides to install such a security system. The setup includes a smart doorbell equipped with a camera, a smart lock system, motion sensors placed strategically around the house, and a control hub to manage them all. Ideally, this system should notify the homeowner of any unusual activity detected by the sensors and offer remote control over the lock and camera feed.

Despite its advantages, this hypothetical scenario could pose a range of challenges. Firstly, the system could become a target for cyberattacks, where malicious actors aim to gain unauthorized access to the house. To counter this, the deployment of stringent security measures, like encryption and two-factor authentication, would be essential. Additionally, the homeowner might have privacy concerns, as this system would collect and store sensitive data related to their household and lifestyle.

On the upside, this smart system could significantly elevate the homeowner's peace of mind, offering features like remote access and real-time alerts. However, on the downside, the requirement for robust security measures could add complexity, requiring a considerable investment of time from the homeowner in understanding the security protocols, using them correctly, and maintaining them over time. Moreover, there might be concerns about how the security of the system could be compromised if it's not managed properly, leading to potential privacy issues.

This scenario underscores the potential benefits and challenges of IoT implementation within the smart home sector. It highlights the importance of robust security features, privacy safeguards, and user-friendly designs in IoT applications. It also underscores the need for user education and awareness to manage these systems effectively and maintain their security and privacy.

B. Case Study 2: Smart Cities

A smart city is a city that uses IoT technology to improve the quality of life for its citizens, enhance sustainability, and optimize resource utilization. One example of smart city technology is the use of sensors to monitor traffic flow and adjust traffic lights accordingly, resulting in reduced congestion and travel time. Smart lighting systems that adjust the brightness and color of streetlights based on the time of day and weather conditions are another example of smart city technology implementation [22].

Smart cities offer several benefits, including improved public safety, reduced traffic congestion, and increased energy efficiency. For example, smart traffic management systems can reduce accidents and improve emergency response times, while smart waste management systems can reduce landfill waste and increase recycling rates. However, the implementation of smart cities also has challenges. One major challenge is the cost of implementation, as it requires significant investment in infrastructure and technology [31]. Another challenge is the privacy and security of citizens, as the collection of data from connected devices can raise concerns about surveillance and data breaches [7].

Hypothetical Implementation Scenario: In a hypothetical metropolis named "TechnoCity", local government has adopted IoT technology city-wide in an attempt to improve the lives of citizens and enhance city management. The city is furnished with connected traffic lights and parking meters, public transportation equipped with IoT devices for real-time tracking, and smart sensors placed throughout the city to monitor air quality, noise, and temperature. The city also employs IoT devices to manage public utilities such as water, electricity, and waste management.

In this hypothetical scenario, the interoperability issue of IoT devices becomes apparent. The city's various IoT devices come from different manufacturers and use different communication protocols, making it difficult for these devices to share data effectively.

Another issue is privacy. The city's IoT devices are constantly collecting data, some of which could infringe upon citizens' privacy rights. For instance, smart meters could reveal personal patterns such as when a home is unoccupied, and real-time tracking on public transport could be used to track the movements of individuals.

TechnoCity also faces potential security challenges. The sheer number of IoT devices in the city creates numerous points of vulnerability. Without robust security measures, these devices could be hacked, leading to manipulation of the city's critical systems.

In terms of scalability and resource constraints, managing and processing the massive amount of data generated by the city's IoT devices is a significant challenge. Moreover, many of these devices operate on batteries and require energy-efficient protocols to ensure continuous operation.

Finally, the cost of implementing, maintaining, and upgrading these IoT systems can be prohibitive, especially considering the scale of a city-wide IoT implementation.

This hypothetical scenario underlines the complex challenges cities could face when integrating IoT technology at a large scale. It also illustrates the interconnected nature of these challenges, emphasizing the need for a comprehensive approach to IoT security and management.

C. Case Study 3: Healthcare

IoT technology has the potential to revolutionize healthcare by enabling remote monitoring, personalized treatment, and real-time data analysis [18]. One example of IoT in healthcare is the use of wearable devices to monitor patients with chronic conditions such as diabetes and heart disease. These devices can track vital signs and alert patients and healthcare providers to potential health problems. Another example is the use of telemedicine, which enables remote consultations and virtual visits with healthcare providers [18].

IoT technology offers several benefits in healthcare, including improved patient outcomes, reduced healthcare costs, and increased access to care. For example, remote monitoring can reduce hospital readmissions and emergency department visits, while telemedicine can improve access to care in rural and underserved areas. However, there are challenges associated with the use of IoT in healthcare. One major challenge is the security and privacy of patient data, as healthcare data is highly sensitive and can be vulnerable to hacking and data breaches [3]. Another challenge is the regulation and standardization of IoT devices in healthcare, as they are subject to strict regulations and quality standards [27].

D. Case Study 4: Agriculture

The IoT holds substantial potential for agricultural advancements. Through the real-time monitoring of crops, soil conditions, and weather patterns, IoT can equip farmers with data-driven insights to make optimal decisions about planting, irrigation, and harvesting. A striking instance of this is the recent adoption of IoT-based precision agriculture systems, which use sensors and devices to monitor soil and weather conditions, and plant growth. These systems leverage the data to optimize resource usage and enhance crop yield [28].

Despite the compelling prospects, the adoption of IoT in agriculture is not without challenges. The significant cost associated with implementing IoT devices presents a formidable barrier, especially for farmers in developing regions. Furthermore, the lack of internet connectivity in many rural regions, where the majority of farming occurs, compounds the problem, potentially exacerbating the digital divide between rural and urban areas [28].

E. Case Study 5: Transportation

IoT technology has the potential to revolutionize transportation by enabling real-time monitoring of vehicles, traffic, and infrastructure. One example is the use of connected vehicles and intelligent transportation systems to improve traffic flow and safety [2]. However, the implementation of IoT devices in transportation faces several challenges, such as the lack of standardization and interoperability of different devices, and the security and privacy concerns associated with the collection of driver and vehicle data. The lack of standardization and interoperability of different devices can create issues of compatibility, making it difficult to integrate different devices into a single system. This can hinder the development of an effective IoT-based transportation system. Additionally, the security and privacy of driver and vehicle data can be vulnerable to hacking and data breaches, leading to potential risks for drivers and passengers [3].

F. In Summary

The case studies and scenarios discussed highlight the transformative potential and challenges of IoT technologies in various sectors, such as efficiency enhancement, improved safety, sustainability, and concerns like privacy, and standardization.

IoT applications in smart homes and cities offer numerous benefits but also present significant security and privacy challenges. These issues necessitate comprehensive solutions, including robust security protocols, privacy-preserving techniques, and user education and awareness, for successful and secure IoT implementation.

Addressing these complexities demands collective effort from policymakers, industry leaders, and researchers. Such efforts can enable responsible and ethical IoT adoption.

Refer to Table II for a summary of each case study, detailing the specific IoT applications within those sectors, their key benefits, and the associated challenges. For the hypothetical implementations and their challenges, refer to Table III which provides a more nuanced explanation of each issue.

V. Comprehensive Solutions to Overcome IoT Security Limitations and Challenges

Addressing IoT security limitations and challenges necessitates a holistic approach encompassing the entire IoT ecosystem. This section presents a set of crucial solutions and recommendations that align with the case studies and discussions previously presented in this paper.

A. Enhancing Standardization and Interoperability

One of the primary challenges across the IoT landscape is the lack of standardization and interoperability among different devices and systems. To address this issue, organizations and governments must collaborate to develop and adopt common standards and protocols [4]. As discussed earlier, initiatives like the NIST Cybersecurity Framework [38], ISO/IEC 21823-1:2019 [11], and GDPR [27] are steps in the right direction. However, further efforts are required to promote the widespread adoption of these standards and ensure seamless integration among IoT devices and systems.

B. Robust Security Measures

IoT devices and systems must incorporate robust security measures to protect against cyber threats and ensure the privacy of users' data [31]. This includes adopting strong encryption, secure authentication, access control mechanisms, and timely software updates. Additionally, organizations must follow security best practices, such as the guidelines provided by the NIST Cybersecurity Framework, to manage cybersecurity risks effectively.

C. Privacy by Design

The "Privacy by Design" concept, originally formulated by Ann Cavoukian in the 1990s, has been touted as a proactive approach to embed privacy into the design specifications of technologies, business practices, and networked infrastructure [6]. It proposes that privacy assurance must ideally become an organization's default mode of operation.

However, beyond being a buzzword or political strategy, the realization of "Privacy by Design" poses scientific and technical challenges. It requires rigorous methodologies in the development process to ensure privacy. This is not a trivial matter in IoT, where devices generate and collect large amounts of personal data continuously and in real-time.

Several aspects contribute to the scientific rigor of "Privacy by Design". First is the incorporation of privacy-enhancing technologies (PETs) during the design phase [8]. PETs, which include encryption techniques, anonymization tools, and differential privacy methods, can help to minimize personal data collection, restrict data processing, and strengthen data security.

Second, a system's architecture must be designed to enforce privacy policies effectively, ensuring that the system behaves as expected even in the face of attacks [33]. This involves techniques such as policy languages and policy enforcement mechanisms, which should be based on sound mathematical foundations to provide provable guarantees.

Third, privacy impact assessments (PIAs) should be conducted routinely throughout the system's lifecycle [39]. PIAs can help to identify potential privacy risks and propose mitigation strategies. They should be based on a comprehensive understanding of privacy principles and legislation, and they should be verified by third-party audits to ensure transparency and accountability.

In conclusion, "Privacy by Design" is not merely a slogan or strategy. Its successful implementation requires scientific rigor and technical expertise, with the commitment to make privacy a default setting in IoT systems. However, such an approach needs to be adopted widely, transcending organizations and sectors, to truly uphold the privacy rights of individuals in the face of growing IoT applications.

D. Education and Awareness

Increasing security awareness among IoT device users can help mitigate risks associated with device misuse or poor security practices [17]. This includes educating users about the potential risks of IoT devices, the importance of regular

TABLE II. SUMMARY OF IOT CASE STUDIES

Case Study	IoT Applications	Key Benefits	Key Challenges
Smart Home Technology	Security Systems, Smart Thermostats	Improved comfort and convenience, safety	Privacy concerns, device compatibility
Smart Cities	Intelligent Traffic Management Systems, Smart Grids	Improved public services, sustainability, quality of life	Scalability, data privacy, infrastructure investment
Healthcare	Remote Patient Monitoring, Wearable Fitness Trackers	Enhanced patient care, reduced healthcare costs, proactive health management	Data security, interoperability, compliance with regulations
Agriculture	Precision Farming, Livestock Monitoring	Optimized resource usage, increased crop yields, efficient farm management	High implementation cost, rural connectivity
Transportation	Connected Cars, Autonomous Vehicles	Improved safety, traffic management, vehicle performance	Safety concerns, real-time data processing, reliability

TABLE III. KEY CHALLENGES IN HYPOTHETICAL IOT IMPLEMENTATIONS

Case Study	Key Challenges	Explanation
Smart Homes	Privacy concerns, need for user education, compatibility and standardization	Privacy issues arise due to extensive data collection and need for secure systems. Interoperability issues occur when devices from different manufacturers don't work together seamlessly. The need for user education arises from the complexities of managing smart home systems.
Smart Cities	Privacy concerns, scalability, need for infrastructure investment, interoperability	Privacy issues arise due to extensive data collection. IoT systems in smart cities need to be scalable to handle increasing data volumes. Large infrastructure investments are needed for smart city implementation. Interoperability among different systems and devices is a crucial requirement.

updates, and best practices for securing their devices. Manufacturers and service providers should invest in user education and training to promote secure IoT usage.

E. Collaboration between Stakeholders

Effective collaboration between stakeholders, including governments, industry leaders, researchers, and end-users, is essential for addressing IoT security challenges [3]. This collaboration can facilitate the sharing of knowledge, resources, and expertise, leading to more effective solutions and strategies for securing IoT devices and systems [1].

F. Leveraging Artificial Intelligence and Machine Learning

Artificial intelligence (AI) and machine learning (ML) techniques have become crucial tools in the realm of IoT security [16], [25]. The data-intensive nature of IoT systems has made traditional security measures inadequate, hence necessitating the use of more sophisticated approaches like AI and ML [35].

AI and ML algorithms can analyze vast amounts of data generated by IoT devices to identify patterns and detect anomalies that may indicate security breaches. This method is often faster and more effective than human monitoring, thus enabling a prompt response and mitigation of threats [16]. Moreover, these algorithms can learn from past incidents and continuously improve their threat detection capabilities, providing a dynamic security solution that adapts to evolving threats [25].

In addition to threat detection, AI and ML can also contribute to IoT security by predicting potential vulnerabilities and proactively strengthening security measures [35]. They can be used to analyze the behavior of devices and networks to identify weak points that could be exploited by malicious actors.

Lastly, AI and ML can play a critical role in managing the complexity of IoT systems. They can help automate security processes, such as authentication and encryption, and manage the increasing number of devices in IoT networks [25]. As a result, AI and ML not only enhance the security of IoT systems but also contribute to their overall efficiency and scalability.

VI. CONCLUSION

This paper has offered an exhaustive analysis of the challenges and limitations of IoT security, spotlighting a wide range of sectors from smart homes to agriculture. We've underscored key challenges—ranging from data privacy, security, the cost of implementation, the absence of standardization, to legal and regulatory hurdles—that pose significant impediments to successful IoT integration across industries. Our review of government standards and frameworks further illustrates the evolving regulatory landscape in IoT security.

However, our research contributes more than a summary of existing knowledge. Our work offers a nuanced understanding of the complex web of issues surrounding IoT security, providing a multi-faceted perspective on the solutions, which weave together technical, legislative, and educational approaches. We've emphasized the importance of a collaborative, multi-stakeholder approach to address IoT security challenges and highlighted the potential of artificial intelligence and machine learning in enhancing IoT security.

In addition to this, our research indicates the need for increased public awareness about IoT security and the development of a culture of cybersecurity among IoT users and developers. Fostering such a culture, combined with industry-wide commitment to IoT security, is integral to building a more resilient and secure IoT ecosystem.

Our findings point to an urgent need for ongoing collaboration between policymakers, industry leaders, and researchers to further standardize and secure IoT technology. As the IoT landscape continues to evolve, these collective efforts are essential for striking a balance between the need for innovation and growth with the protection of users' rights and interests.

In summary, while IoT technology brings forth immense opportunities for innovation and growth, it is paramount that we acknowledge and address the inherent security challenges. By understanding these challenges and working collaboratively to surmount them, we can harness the full potential of IoT and pave the way for a more interconnected, efficient, and secure world.

REFERENCES

[1] Mohammad Aazam, Marc St-Hilaire, and Chung-Horng Lung. IoT standards, protocols and security. *IEEE Access*, 7:129551–129571, 2019.

[2] Mohammad Aazam, Sherali Zeadally, and Khaled A Harras. Deploying fog computing in industrial internet of things and industry 4.0. *IEEE Transactions on Industrial Informatics*, 14(10):4674–4682, 2018.

[3] Ala Al-Fuqaha, Mohsen Guizani, and Kemal Akkaya. Internet of Things: A survey on enabling technologies, protocols, and applications. *IEEE Communications Surveys & Tutorials*, 2022.

[4] Cesare Alippi and Giusy Vanini. Adaptive IoT solutions with energy harvesting. In Ovidiu Vermesan and Joël Bacquet, editors, *IoT Enablers: Technologies and Implementation*, pages 203–239. River Publishers, 2019.

[5] Luigi Atzori, Antonio Iera, and Giacomo Morabito. The Internet of Things: A survey. *Computer Networks*, 54(15):2787–2805, 2010.

[6] Ann Cavoukian. *Privacy by Design: The 7 Foundational Principles*. Information and Privacy Commissioner of Ontario, Canada, 2009.

[7] Jie Chen, Yishuang Huang, and Yajie Qin. A comprehensive review on the cost-effectiveness of IoT technologies. *IEEE Access*, 10:27437–27453, 2022.

[8] George Danezis, Josep Domingo-Ferrer, Marit Hansen, Jaap-Henk Hoepman, Daniel Le Métayer, Rodica Tirtea, and Stefan Schiffner. Privacy-preserving data mining. In *Handbook of Information and Communication Security*, pages 615–634. Springer, 2010.

[9] Michel Girard. *Standards for Cybersecure IoT Devices: A Way Forward*. Centre for International Governance Innovation, 2020.

[10] Saurabh Gupta, Rakesh Goyal, and Gurpreet Singh. Scalability in IoT: A review. *Journal of Information Processing Systems*, 17(4):988–1005, 2021.

[11] ISO. ISO/IEC 21823-1:2019 Internet of Things (IoT) — interoperability for IoT systems — part 1: Framework. https://www.iso.org/standard/71885.html, 2019. Accessed on May 29, 2023.

[12] ISO. ISO/IEC 27001 – information security management systems. https://www.iso.org/standard/54534.html, 2022. Accessed on March 16, 2023.

[13] ISO. ISO/IEC 27002:2022 – information security, cybersecurity and privacy protection — information security controls. https://www.iso.org/standard/75652.html, 2022. Accessed on March 16, 2023.

[14] Robert Johnson, Maria Nguyen, and Raj Patel. Cross-border data flows in IoT: Legal challenges and solutions. *Journal of International Law and Technology*, 7(2):234–257, 2022.

[15] Nickson M Karie, Nor Masri Sahri, Wencheng Yang, Craig Valli, and Victor R Kebande. A review of security standards and frameworks for iot-based smart environments. *IEEE Access*, 9:121975–121995, 2021.

[16] Minhaj Ahmad Khan and Khaled Salah. IoT security: Review, blockchain solutions, and open challenges. *Future generation computer systems*, 82:395–411, 2018.

[17] Constantinos Kolias, Georgios Kambourakis, Angelos Stavrou, and Jeffrey Voas. Ddos in the IoT: Mirai and other botnets. *Computer*, 50(7):80–84, 2017.

[18] Shancang Li, Houbing Song, and Muddesar Iqbal. Privacy and security for resource-constrained iot devices and networks: Research challenges and opportunities. *Sensors*, 19(8), 2019.

[19] Li Lin, Xiaofei Liao, Hai Jin, and Peng Li. Computation offloading toward edge computing. *Proceedings of the IEEE*, 107(8):1584–1607, 2019.

[20] Xiao Liu, Yu Chen, Zhen Wang, and Wei Zhang. Security and privacy in IoT: Challenges, solutions, and future directions. *IEEE Communications Surveys & Tutorials*, 24(1):789–823, 2022.

[21] Rwan Mahmoud, Tasneem Yousuf, Fadi Aloul, and Imran Zualkernan. Internet of Things (IoT) security: Current status, challenges and prospective measures. In *2015 10th international conference for internet technology and secured transactions (ICITST)*, pages 336–341. IEEE, 2015.

[22] Imran Makhdoom, Mehran Abolhasan, Justin Lipman, Ren Ping Liu, and Wei Ni. Anatomy of threats to the internet of things. *IEEE Communications Surveys & Tutorials*, 21(2):1636–1675, 2019.

[23] André Mayer, Vinicius Rodrigues, Cristiano André da Costa, Rodrigo Righi, Alex Roehrs, and Rodolfo Antunes. FogChain: A fog computing architecture integrating blockchain and internet of things for personal health records. *IEEE Access*, PP:1–1, 09 2021.

[24] Yang Ming and Tingting Zhang. Efficient privacy-preserving access control scheme in electronic health records system. *Sensors*, 18(10), 2018.

[25] Mehdi Mohammadi, Ala Al-Fuqaha, Sameh Sorour, and Mohsen Guizani. Deep learning for IoT big data and streaming analytics: A survey. *IEEE Communications Surveys & Tutorials*, 20(4):2923–2960, 2018.

[26] Mahda Noura, Mohammed Atiquzzaman, and Martin Gaedke. Interoperability in internet of things: Taxonomies and open challenges. *Mobile networks and applications*, 24:796–809, 2019.

[27] European Parliament and Council. Regulation (EU) 2016/679 of the european parliament and of the council of 27 april 2016 on the protection of natural persons with regard to the processing of personal data and on the free movement of such data, and repealing directive 95/46/EC (general data protection regulation). https://eur-lex.europa.eu/eli/reg/2016/679/oj, 2016.

[28] Sameer Qazi, Bilal A. Khawaja, and Qazi Umar Farooq. IoT-equipped and AI-enabled next generation smart agriculture: A critical review, current challenges and future trends. *IEEE Access*, 10:21219–21235, 2022.

[29] Sina Shahhosseini, Arman Anzanpour, Iman Azimi, Sina Labbaf, DongJoo Seo, Sung-Soo Lim, Pasi Liljeberg, Nikil Dutt, and Amir M Rahmani. Exploring computation offloading in IoT systems. *Information Systems*, 107:101860, 2022.

[30] Gabi Siboni and Tal Koren. *The Threat of Connected Devices to the Internet*. Institute for National Security Studies, 2016.

[31] Rishi S. Sinha, Ying Wei, and Seong H. Hwang. A review on low power IoT devices and applications. *Electronics*, 10(11):1314, 2021.

[32] John Smith, Alice Brown, and Ethan Miller. Resource management in IoT networks: Recent advances and challenges. *IEEE Communications Surveys & Tutorials*, 2022.

[33] Sarah Spiekermann and Lorrie Faith Cranor. Privacy by design: the definitive workshop. *Identity in the Information Society*, 2(2):243–254, 2009.

[34] Sarah Thompson, Brian Lee, and Carlos Silva. Developing legal frameworks for IoT: Balancing innovation and regulation. *International Journal of Law and Information Technology*, 31(1):78–101, 2023.

[35] Nazar Waheed, Xiangjian He, Muhammad Ikram, Muhammad Usman, Saad Sajid Hashmi, and Muhammad Usman. Security and privacy in iot using machine learning and blockchain: Threats and countermeasures. *ACM Comput. Surv.*, 53(6), dec 2020.

[36] Chao Wang, Jie Xu, Hong Zhang, Yang Zhang, and Tao Li. Edge computing for IoT: A comprehensive survey. *ACM Computing Surveys (CSUR)*, 56(1):1–40, 2023.

[37] Jiajie Wang, Zhenyu Zhang, Yuyu Zhang, and Yun Chen. Internet of Things (IoT) based personalized healthcare system. *J. Med. Syst.*, 42(4):70, 2018.

[38] James Webb and Dustin Hume. Campus IoT collaboration and governance using the nist cybersecurity framework. In *Living in the Internet of Things: Cybersecurity of the IoT-2018*, pages 1–7. IET, 2018.

[39] David Wright and Paul De Hert. The relationship between privacy impact assessments and risk management. *Risk management: an international journal*, 14(3):206–221, 2012.

[40] Ibrar Yaqoob, Ibrahim Abaker Targio Hashem, Abdullah Gani, Salimah Mokhtar, Ejaz Ahmed, Nor Badrul Anuar, and Athanasios V Vasilakos. Big data: From beginning to future. *International Journal of Information Management*, 36(6):1231–1247, 2016.